D0049979

Jesus Laughed and Other Reflections on Being Human

Jean Maalouf

Sheed & Ward
Kansas City

Copyright© 1996 by Jean Maalouf

All rights reserved. Except as permitted under the Copyright Act of 1976, no part of this book may be reproduced or transmitted in any form or by any means, electronic or mechanical, including photocopying, recording or by an information storage and retrieval system without permission in writing from the Publisher.

Sheed & Ward™ is a service of The National Catholic Reporter Publishing Company.

Library of Congress Cataloging-in-Publication Data
Maalouf, Jean.
    Jesus laughed and other reflections on being human
/ Jean Maalouf.
        p.   cm.
    ISBN: 1-55612-911-4
    1. Jesus Christ--Devotional literature.   2. Spiritual
life--Catholic Church.   3. Catholic Church--Doctrines.
I. Title.
BT306.5.M23   1996
242--dc20   96-32973
                                                      CIP

Published by: Sheed & Ward
               115 E. Armour Blvd.
               P.O. Box 419492
               Kansas City, MO 64141-6492

To order, call: (800) 333-7373

Cover illustration and design by Jane Pitz.

Contents

To the kindred in spirit and the beloved in Him: Joan, Ruth, Georgia, Kristen, Nancy, Robert, Andy, Beatrice, and Rogers, who, with great generosity of their time and heart, assisted me, in various ways, to write this book, with love and gratitude.

With that their eyes opened and they recognized
Him; whereupon He vanished from their sight.

               – Luke 24:31

The fact is that whether you eat or drink –
whatever you do – you should do all for the
glory of God.

               – 1 Corinthians 10:31

Spirituality is not to be learned by flight from
the world . . . We must learn to penetrate
things and find God there.

               – Meister Eckhart

My Beloved is the mountains,
And lonely wooded valleys,
Strange Islands,
And resounding rivers
The whistling of love-stirring breezes,
the tranquil night
At the time of rising dawn,
Silent solitude.
The supper that refreshes and deepens love.

               – John of the Cross

What good is it to me if Mary gave birth to the
Son of God fourteen hundred years ago and I
do not also give birth to the Son of God in my
time and in my culture?

               – Meister Eckhart

When we say God is "eternal," we mean God is
eternally young.

               – Meister Eckhart

The glory of God is a human being who is fully
alive!

               – Saint Ireneaus

ℰᴑ

Prologue

A Welcoming Invitation

Jesus is still less known than we think, even though millions of books have been written about Him.

Are we really aware of the fact that He was fully divine and fully human? Do we really know that He showed us how much God was magnetic and vulnerable? Do we really know that, in Him, the Word of God moved into the very center of human existence and became flesh, one of us? Do we really know that He had a great sense of humor, He laughed, He cried, He was anxious, He had friends, He went to parties, He was furious at the hypocrites and the liars, He was a rebel, He felt tired, abandoned and betrayed, He loved people, He liked solitude, silence and the beauty of nature, He loved life, He was like you and me? Do we really know that the best way to find God is through our own humanity, that the best way to be God-like is to become more fully human, and that the best way to be fully human is to live the Word in human flesh? Do we really know that the Incarnation is not only that historical event that happened some 2000 years ago, but it is a continuous happening? Do we really know that, because of His continuous Presence among us, we should be able to celebrate a continuous Christmas? Do we really know that, in Him, we "have strength for everything" (Philippians 4:13)?

We may know all this theoretically. But do we really know it existentially? Does what we know of Jesus makes *the* difference in our lives? Do we live by what we know of Jesus? If you read this book with an open mind and heart, expect that you will change. Expect then to grow. Just allow Him to work with you, within you. He will touch the very roots of your consciousness, and you will certainly have new ways of thinking, seeing, feeling, behaving, loving – living. Expect to "have strength for everything." Expect to live life to its fullest.

What I am sharing with you in this book has changed my life. I promise it will change your life too. Who can resist the flame of a living Christ?

Let me tell you what I mean. Please read on.

$\wp$

Introduction

Have you heard about the Magical City? The story begins: There was a man who got sick and tired of life as it was. He was tired of his family, his friends, and of his work. He was tired of pleasures. He was tired of the routine of having to repeat the same thing over and over every day. So one day, he decided to leave everything behind him. He left his family, his friends, his work, his inheritance, his heritage, his home town, everything, everything, and went out into the open air and the open field, looking for something else. He was searching for something like the perfect city or the Magical City, where everything would be different, exciting, new and fascinating. So, he left.

On his journey, he somehow ended up in a forest. It was already nighttime. He ate a cheese sandwich and an apple, and took off his shoes. Very carefully, he pointed them in the new direction, the direction in which he was headed. He let go of his worries and he went to sleep. The next morning, he stepped into his shoes, and he continued his journey toward the direction of the Magical City. He was unaware of what had happened during his sleep. In fact, during the night, his shoes were turned around by a playful animal. After a few days, the man arrived to the Magical City. But, to his surprise, the Magical City was not very different from his home town. It looked very familiar. There were familiar streets, familiar stores, familiar houses, familiar faces. He knocked at a familiar door, and he found more familiar faces. He lived there happily ever after.

I thought that this little story would illustrate what you are going to read about in this book. The magic is to be found in the ordinary, the familiar, the everyday life. That which is magical does not enter your life from somewhere outside. Rather, that which is outside becomes magical, because of an internal change in you – a change which has caused you to see the same things in a different light. Why? Precisely because God is where you are living, in the earthiness of the here and now. Stop looking elsewhere for God.

This book is about spirituality. You may add whatever adjective you wish to this word and say, for instance: Incarnational spirituality, existential spirituality, holistic spirituality, enfleshed spirituality, experiential spirituality, practical spirituality, global spirituality, integrated spirituality, process spirituality, secular holiness, or even spirituality of the real. The underlying concept of the book is the realization – not in a speculative way, but in a very concrete way – that God is involved here and now in what you are doing; that any philosophy or spirituality for which the attainment of a state of perfection demands asceticism, withdrawal from the world, or self-denial – even though it may have had its merits sometime in the course of human history – has now disappeared, or is, at least, in its way out in this modern age. The new spirituality is the spirituality of the divine/human integration and of the here and now. It's one that embraces *both* the sacred *and* the secular, the holy matter rather than the spirit vs. matter, the "is" rather than the "should," the God made flesh in the Incarnation which is still continuing rather than the remote God.

This "new" realization of spirituality is, in fact, not new. It has existed since the beginning of time. In Genesis, it is said: "God looked at everything he had made, and he found it very good" (Genesis 1:31). It is not said that God did a very good job, but that *it was very good*. What is new is that our perspective has changed. We have now new eyes for seeing life. If in the past, the Greeks saw the dawn of reason, we are seeing, now, the dawning of new spiritual life, not only in individuals, but in the human family as a whole.

A new spiritual consciousness is taking shape based on that transforming magical energy called love. It transforms the ordinary into the extraordinary. No one has described more humanly than Jesus, the dynamics of the Kingdom of God, which is not a system, nor a set of rules, or some physical, psychological or political force, but rather love in the concrete situations we are living in. Love is the deepest and the most compelling of all human powers. To embrace Jesus' definition of love, we have to let go of our own notions of false realities. Perhaps even more painfully, We must let go of our incomplete understandings and the patterns of thought which we carefully developed in the course of our lives thus far. These patterns are not only personal, but also collective, belonging as they do to the human family as a whole. We must accept the fact that the Spirit is guiding the creation along, in its various stages of evolution, through the evolving consciousness of human beings. Love is also an invitation to let go – and how painful it is! – even of the temples we have so proudly built. The temples of stones and especially the temples of the mind, built with their gorgeous cathedrals of dogma and thought, must be re-evaluated, not because they were false or not good – Ah! God, no! – but because our interpretations of reality have changed, and we have arrived at different understandings. Even when it comes to the Gospel, we have developed new understandings of God's truths and a different mode of preaching the Gospel and living it.

It has taken a long, long time for us to realize that building the most beautiful cathedrals, waging the most holy

wars, embarking on crusades and inquisitions, or excom-
municating all who do not profess our view of faith . . .
are not the best ways to preach to Gospel, no matter how
well-intentioned or morally justifiable some of these actions
may have seemed at one time or another. There is a more
direct and effective way of doing it today. Living it. Loving
our neighbor. Giving, with love, a little glass of water to
someone thirsty. Visiting, with great love, the sick. Assisting,
with great love, the needy. Helping, with great love, to
liberate an oppressed. Being open to others. Engaging in
dialogue. (Dialogue is a great discovery in our modern world.)
We do not solve problems through wars and bloodshed.
We can solve them by talking and listening and working
things out in an atmosphere of good will. Dialogue is a
basic need between nations, just as it is between husband
and wife, parents and children, teacher and student, lover
and beloved, rich and poor, management and labor. And
listening, listening, listening without prejudice. Isn't this the
most effective way to preach the Gospel? A shifting to the
real love is urgent. Where institutions do not fit, Jesus
certainly does.

This book is therefore an invitation to take a close
look at Jesus of Nazareth, who is the message in flesh and
blood. Jesus invested so much in the spiritual, but also in
the temporal. He says what He is, and He is what He says.
He is the stuff of the Spirit/Body. How can we reject the
Spirit at the expense of the Body, or vice versa? In a sense,
theology and philosophy have missed Jesus somehow. They
talk about Him eloquently and wonderfully, but they miss
the man, Jesus. We need not study merely the biography
of Jesus. Rather, we need to discover Him living now, in
our everyday life. In Jesus, God has become a human reality:
the Beyond in our midst – an existential Transcendence.
God is not impressed by our eruditions. Nor is God tamed
by our theological speculations, nor by our churches, our

managerial skills, even our prayers. Words are supposed to speak, but words say little. The Word does not philosophize or theologize. The Word lives, loves, comforts, heals, inspires, transforms. It is a living experience: "And the life I live now is not my own; Christ is living in me" (Galatians 2:20). When we come to recognize God as the active agent in our lives, we become less rigid in many areas of our behavior, and more willing to surrender to the workings of the Holy Spirit in us. To say that we know God is one thing; but to live the experiential realization of this knowing – to live God existentially – is quite another, indeed.

Hence the need for new saints. We need new forms of asceticism and mysticism, with a new agenda for the century at its beginning. This new agenda would have characteristics such as the following: holistic and global spirituality, no labels whatsoever (conservative, liberal, rightist, leftist . . . are all false, because they are mere constructs of the mind); no prejudices whatsoever; a realization that creation was left unfinished, and that God's final Word to us is the power He has given us to co-create with Him, because it was not His intention to create everything at once; an acknowledgment that human beings are more important than theology; and a conviction that liberation is not something which comes about in archives and libraries, or through transfer of power, but rather that liberation takes place within one's own heart, and that what one does to oneself or to others, one does it to Christ Himself.

In a sense, Christianity has failed to convey a full understanding of the true God to the world. God is not "The Man Upstairs," or "The Big Executive," or "The Magician" who makes things happen. God is infinitely attractive and vulnerable. He is Christ, in His most appealing divine/human form. To think, act, love as Christ does, and to experience Him and to identify with Him, to actually be Him, is what Christianity is all about. It is to experience

God, not by hearsay, but in a real, concrete, palpable way. Being fully human is the most real and, at the same time, the most sacred way to be a Christ. Spiritual life is not simply a mere idealistic noble concept. It is something very real. This book is therefore about reality.

The bottom line of all this is the firm conviction that God is here and now. The Incarnation, which continues to happen everyday, has changed the whole gestalt of modern spirituality. The separation between the sacred and the secular, the divine and the human, is an invention of the human mind, and is therefore fictitious. This is why "both/and" corresponds more than "either/or" to what we call reality.

My intention is to help provide a certain spiritual climate (a "spiritual ecology") in which the divine becomes the main drive for the expansion of the human consciousness and love becomes the natural path to God. A new world order demands a radical change in our consciousness. We need a new way of seeing everything. We need an awakening. We need a new approach to spirituality, more centered on the Word, living here and now in the community to which we happen to belong. The communion of the community – be it the Church or any other form of togetherness – is the essential element of this spirituality. It is the element to be nurtured, the element to which we should direct our energy and loyalty. Institutions, structures and rituals as such, are secondary and somewhat extraneous. I also intend to answer, in one way or another, two challenging questions: What if the "God of the ordinary" were considered to be one and the same as the "God of the extraordinary"? And what if the God of the marketplace were different from the God which is found in the existing, man-made "marketplace" of religions?

This book conveys a number of theological, philosophical and psychological ideas. It is written in a simple, direct, and often poetic language, with a view to reaching a large audience and making a difference in the lives of many. What is said may sometimes seem annoying and trenchant, other times perplexing or exacting, and most of the time is thought provoking. But who ever said that God's way is just the way of compromise and appeasement? The Word of God does not work like a drug, but rather like a seed. A seed, when growing, can even move a rock, the way faith can move a mountain.

So, do not expect to find in this book ready-made answers. Do not approach it as a "how-to" book either. Rather, read it with an open mind, once you have decided to drop shortsighted expectations as well as all sorts of prejudices. Expectations and prejudices can be, and sometimes are, the root of problems when it comes to spiritual life. This book points to ends without lingering on the means that bring them about. It is like an instrument, a flashlight that shows you what, where, how things are. You may use it at your bedside, in your car, while traveling, doubting, worrying, searching, exploring, making decisions, relaxing, and especially when you are in the darkness of your life. A flashlight is not meant to be kept in the warehouse; a flashlight is intended to help you to get to the warehouse. It helps you to detect, and to observe, and to discern what is really there and what really makes sense at that moment.

God is right here and now, involved in whatever we are doing in the here and now. There is no longer any reason to burden our shoulders, alone. We are never alone. Theologians talk about theology, ordinary people of spirituality, live it. The magic of the ordinary is that we meet with Him at every turn, every step of our journey.

℘

1

Incarnation

It is difficult, very difficult, to comprehend – and especially to admit – the Incarnation.

God chose to become a man. He became human, one of us, every one of us, including my neighbor and my enemy. He became present, alive, here and now. Somehow, even if we know that, we have the tendency to send Him back to His heaven, to His divine home. A sage from the Far East says that the majority of Christians understand only half of the Christian message. They understand that God and Christ are one, that Christ is God. But they can't understand that Christ and men are one, that Christ was man and remained man.

But if God were really among us, we would have to risk our tranquillity and our "security." It is indeed easier to stay as we are. Thus it is more comfortable to put God far away.

The message of the Incarnation is that God took our nature in order that we might become like Him, that we might become capable of a new life and become new persons. Christ was born into the world and assumed our nature so that we might be reborn in to His. Christmas is not a birthday party for Christ. It is not a mere remembrance or nostalgic religious practice in observance of an event that occurred some 2000 years ago. Christmas is the birth of Christ at *that* time as well as the birth of Christ in *our* time, *our* culture, *our* selves. Continuing birth. The Word is contemporary and remains among us. Christ uses our face, our hands, our feet, our selves. He is in everyone. He is everyone. He is no longer limited. He became universal. He is hungry now, and thirsty, naked, sick, a stranger, a prisoner. "As often as you did it for one of my least brothers, you did it for me" (Matthew 25:40). We are His members. We are Christ by participation. He reveals Himself all the time in the form of the man or the woman praying in church or walking along the street. He is at the office, at the workshop, on the bus, on the subway, on the plane, in the department store, in the line of people who stand waiting their turn and in those who hurry by on their way. Saint John Chrysostom tells us that the living and human altar on every street is more sacred than a stone altar, because on the latter Christ is offered, but the former is Christ Himself.

Here is a basic heresy: the loss of the sense that sees every other human being as Christ and treats him like Christ. For, as Saint John said, "If anyone says 'my love is fixed on God' yet hates his brother, he is a liar. One who has no love for the brother he has seen cannot love the God he has not seen" (1 John 4:20). Christ is multidimentional. To be aware of His "full stature" (Ephesians 4:13) and to discover all His infinite dimensions, we need to turn upside down the scale of all the values that we have "piously" manufactured. It is a very shaking thing to hear something like "you are only as close to God as you are to your neighbor." So all your prayers and gifts mean nothing if in your heart you have something against your brother.

The Incarnation is a very disturbing reality. It is still "indigestible" and remains the butt of all heresies, a cross

for all spiritualities and traditions, because it does not permit
expression in the spiritual only, nor does it allow contain-
ment in the human only, but it demands interaction between
the divine and the earthly.

The Incarnation was a scandal for the Jews: how was
it possible to lower the invisible into the visible, the Creator
God into created matter?!

The Incarnation was a foolish thing for the Greeks:
how was it possible to place the eternal in time, the spirit
in matter, the one in the many, the universal in the particular?! The Incarnation followed the opposite direction of
Greek idealism, which seeks salvation in "disincarnation."

The Incrnation was difficult, if not impossible, to admit,
for the Ebionites and the followers of Manichaeism, Arian-
ism, Nestorianism, Monophysitism, Monothelitism, and Do-
cetism.

These heresies did not exist only in the past. They
are still alive and well. Look around. Do we truly believe
in the real union between man and God? What if my neighbor
were God? Is there any distinction between love for God
and love for neighbor? For Jesus, the second commandment
is like the first (Matthew 22:37-40). With the Incarnation,
love is not only a kind of human brotherhood or a kind of
simple philanthropy; it becomes much more than that: a
theological virtue that has only one formal object – God –
and one way – the other. The most direct way to reach
God is to reach out to our neighbor. To anyone. Christ was
an example of this "anyone." The disciples of Emmaus
walked with Him for several kilometers without recognizing
Him. He was merely an example of this "anyone." Mary
Magdalene thought He was the gardener but recognized
Him when He said, "Go to my brothers" (John 20:17).

The Incarnation is the passion of God. It is that intense
divine being acting in the here and now. It is God in the
ordinary, God in our day-to-day lives, God hidden in *every*

person we meet in our daily life. He was there, in Nazareth, for thirty years, and few knew Him.

God living today on earth! It is scary. An "earthquake." A terrible presence. It is a catastrophe to fall into the hands of the living God. All our hypocrisies would have to fall too.

The most subtle and sophisticated enemy of the Incarnation is the Pharisee, the individual who, in the name of an ardent zeal for God, turns his face from the God-man/woman. The Pharisee thinks that he is maintaining the best relationship with God when he does not care for his neighbor. He "disincarnates" God. He "purifies" Christ of His body. He expatriates Him to heaven. And this is the most dangerous heresy of our time. How many among us are still Monophysitic without knowing it?

Christ has unified forever, in His person, God and the individual, the vertical and the horizontal dimensions. The true cult for God became the cult for every human being. Our call, therefore, is to embody Christ in us, to give Him birth again and again, to let Him see with our eyes, hear with our ears, walk with our feet, work with our hands. Christ has no other body than ours. It is up to us to prove His birth. Shame on any religion that seeks to prove its credibility by means of the past. The books of history, the tons of research and study prove nothing if the hungry remain hungry, the thirsty remain thirsty, the sick remain sick, prisoners remain incarcerated, the greedy remain greedy, and terrorists continue in their terrorist activities.

The birth of Christ means nothing if it is not a continuing birth. It is up to us, in our own time and place, to invent the Incarnation again and again. Every follower of Christ has to put Christ into the world. Christmas is a passing, empty event if it is only another party. Christmas must be a celebration for another gesture of love and transformation. God has no other way to manifest Himself than by transforming us. And the best way to be Christlike is to be more human, like Him. The birth of Christ is nothing but our birth to a new understanding, a new way of thinking, and new way of living in the world, the way of Christ. For Christ is not simply an object of contemplation and love. He is also "the way, and the truth, and the life" (John 14:6). The Nativity message is not only the message of just another joy, but the biggest joy, the joy of the eschatological fulfillment that we seek in our depths, that all the people of the world have always expected without knowing what it really was. The Incarnation is the infusion of the divine potential into the sphere of human possibilities. The early Fathers put it this way: God became man so that man might become God. Christ is born in our nature so that we may be reborn in the likeness of God. Christmas is the revelation and celebration of the new age for the world and for us.

What I understand from Jesus is that we cannot meet God except in the ordinariness of people and things. This is how they become sacred and unique.

The Incarnation makes me more human. And perhaps the only way to contemplate the wonders of God is to explore the depth of the human being, which is the very ground of divinity. To be more human is, in a sense, to be more divine.

The adventure of the true disciple of the incarnate Christ is to live an intelligent faith in order to know, search for, seek Christ behind the masks that everyone uses to protect himself from everyone else, and from Him too. Christ is born when we get rid of all these masks and become our true selves, when we recover our likeness of God and when we become other Christs.

℘

2

Jesus Was Fully Human – Are You?

Jesus was an authentic man. He lived like a man. He loved living like a man. He laughed like a man. He cried like a man. He was a man, yet, He was the divine Son of God. He was fully human and fully divine.

But why, for heaven's sake, do some people make of Him a myth? They know four things of Him. First, His birth through a virgin. Second, His life of incredible miracles. Third, His painful cross. Fourth, His glorious resurrection. They are missing the real man, Jesus.

Jesus was, above all, a lover. His path was the path of love – love of God and love of all existence. He didn't act through laws of discipline and morality. He acted from His heart. He was so spontaneous, so free, so flowing, so open, so natural. He was like a flower. When a flower opens, the fragrance of it spreads. It cannot be otherwise. He didn't need a cultivated character. A cultivated character is frozen, blocked, paralyzed, immobile. It is like a plastic flower.

You cannot argue with Jesus. He does not follow the rules of logic. He goes beyond logical living. Jesus is a lover – a lover of God and of God's whole existence.

6

Can you understand a lover through logic? Impossible. Love is illogical. Lovers are roundabout. Jesus was roundabout. He used the language of love. He spoke in parables, in stories, in metaphors, in poetry. His words were filled with loving thoughts, enthusiasm, zeal, and inspirations.

You cannot read a mathematical equation again and again. Once it is understood, it is finished. But Jesus' sayings you must read again and again and again, every day. Always, there is something new surfacing because you are transformed by His words and you become more able to see more. The Scripture would allow you to grow within. And when you grow within, the Scripture grows with you. Jesus' words have an eternal quality. The depth of their wisdom is bottomless. Yet He was talking to simple, uneducated people – the farmer, the fisherman, the prostitute, the sinner. And each one understood.

Ordinary people have special qualities. They have special ways of understanding and relating to Jesus, that scholars, professors and high priests perhaps have not. They *trust*. People who live with nature have more trust than others. A community that is less industrialized, less mechanized, and that lives with nature counts more on trust as a way of life. When a farmer sows seeds in his field, he trusts they will sprout when the right season comes. He does not doubt. He simply waits. Only with trust can you understand Jesus! Ordinary people have always known the language of love. They have always understood the language of laughter, tears, dances, songs, and deep breaths. Jesus was human. He was the man of love, of intense human-divine love. He loved this earth. He saw God materialized in His creatures. God – like humanity – is not an abstract concept. You never come across "humanity." You meet this or that human being. You never come across God. You meet Him incarnated in everyone and everything. You feel the immensity of being when you go through the narrow door of this

particular person, this particular tree, or this particular rock
and truly enjoy each one. If you are unable to enjoy life as
it is, you probably will not be able to enjoy God as He is.
Jesus was more human and humane, more affection-
ate, more sensitive than the most delicate one among us.
He was very earthy. He depended on earth stories, parables,
to convey His message of the Kingdom of God. He observed
seeds growing. He compared the Kingdom to the mustard
plant in which birds nest and sing. He asked his followers
to learn basic spiritual lessons from the plants. It is "by
their fruits" that you will distinguish true spiritual people.
He compared Himself to the vine and His disciples to its
branches. They also must be the rich soil where God's seeds
can grow. He liked animals, treated them with respect,
observed them very closely, and learned from them. He
used them as symbols for the reign of God on earth. "The
birds of the air," the "sparrow falling from its nest," the
fishes gathering, the one lost sheep, and all Jesus' parables
that include animals reveal His great sensitivity toward them,
as well as His conviction of the interdependence, the ecology
we share with all living creatures. Indeed, He was born in
a stable among accepting animals, and He died as the "slain
lamb of God."

Jesus was open to His environment. He was close to
it and intimate with it. He contacted people from other
convictions and cultures – Samaritans, pagans, and Romans.
He was especially interested in the oppressed, the neglected,
the isolated, the sick, the poor, and the unwanted. He broke
the barriers that were supposed to prevent Him from talking
with people he was not supposed to talk to. He related to
the old and the young, the able and the disabled. He related
not only to human beings but also to his whole environment.
His words and deeds were filled with references to birds
and fishes, sky and sea, foxes, doves, camels, donkeys,
snakes, sparrows, seeds, grass, lilies, wines, sun and moon,

rocks, sand, lakes, coins, pearls, water, salt, yeast, light, fire, darkness, and bread and wine. The gospels are filled with the open door to nature and the great outdoors. Jesus used our raw materials, enjoyed them and sacralized them. He looked through everything and saw in everything the divine reality of God's living presence. Jesus trusted, "Father, not my will but yours be done" (Luke 22:42).

Jesus lived life intensely and prayerfully. He loved eating, drinking, partying, the company of His friends. He loved the small joys of life. His earth was not rejected by Him. It was rather celebrated. He delighted in this earth. He was a very earth-rooted man. He was superhuman. But sometimes He was also emotionally fragile, weak, helpless – like us. He is very appealing. You can become a fellow traveler with Him. You can be His friend. You can hold His hand. You can eat at the same table with Him and drink from the same pot. He does not ask you to have a dry, sterile life, complicated by unnecessary problems. He wants you to accept all that life gives you. He wants you to be a living person, living an ordinary life. He Himself moved with simple people. For Him, these were the real people because they live with nature. With nature you are natural; you can trust. If you are surrounded only by unnatural things, chances are you become unnatural too. He was Himself son of a carpenter, uneducated, not knowing the sophistication of science and the laws of physics and mathematics. He did not have any degree. His resume must not have been impressive at all. He had all of divine wisdom, without factual knowledge. He had a sense of beauty, without following the rules of aesthetics. He was a poet, without a pen. He reached the Ultimate. With the Ultimate, you cannot be other than the poet. With the Ultimate, you can talk about mysteries in metaphor. The language of mathematics is very exact, hence very narrow. It does not fit life. Neither the language of philosophy, nor the one of theology. Only poets can be close to the truth of God's mysteries.

Jesus lived life intensely and profoundly. He was a real person, fully human and fully Divine. Jesus was a walking mystery. Have you met Him – today? I have!

ॐ

3

Jesus Laughed – Do You?

Could Jesus have been fully human and fully divine without ever having laughed?

This is impossible. Who can then laugh? For some reason, the Christian tradition pictures Jesus as a serious person – perhaps too serious. Some Christians view Him this way because only around this seriousness could they build their serious business. But of course Jesus laughed. He must have enjoyed life – drinking, eating, resting, celebrating with friends. He must have loved life. You may not hear His laughter because His laughter was very subtle and deeply profound in life's contradictions. Jesus was a light-hearted man. He lived with all His heart and out of His depth of being. He enjoyed all things in life, even the smallest. He didn't renounce life. He made life and living sacred. He was a very joyful man, a man of celebrations. When you go to see Him, you will see Him, when not in prayer, at a dining table, relaxing with friends. He enjoyed eating. He even made eating sacramental, a way of prayer. He made prayers of all human actions. He drank wine. He allowed His disciples to drink wine also. Life is ecstasy, and the wine became the symbol of ecstasy. Wine is not a need, it is a celebration of life. Life is not the fulfillment of needs, nor duties, nor performances. Rather, life is a dance, an art, a poem. But is this the way to become a "saint"? That perhaps is why he was condemned, crucified. The cross, ironically, became a symbol of Christianity and a symbol of seriousness – a dead seriousness. Because of the cross and the crucified Jesus, most people think unconsciously that sadness must be virtuous and they live against life, forgetting that God is "the God of the living, not of the dead" (Matthew 22:32). They condemn the wonders of all that is life. They think life is sinful. How far are they from what Jesus recommends: "Be glad and rejoice" (Matthew 5:12). "I shall see you again; then your hearts will rejoice with a joy no one can take from you" (John 16:22). At the Last Supper, even when He was about to be betrayed, arrested, cursed, beaten, humiliated, rejected, mortified, and crucified, He talked about joy to his disciples by saying, "All this I tell you that my joy may be yours and your joy may be complete" (John 15:11).

Is it conceivable that Jesus, for example, didn't smile at those little children whom He allowed to come and sit down and maybe play with Him? And is it conceivable that He didn't have a friendly smile for His disciples and for all the people who came to Him? And is it conceivable that He didn't laugh with His family and closest friends at life's incongruities? And how, without laughter, could He attend parties, eating and drinking, and mixing with different people?

Jesus had a very subtle laughter – you may not even hear it, but He laughed. He was delighted with life – even if you do not see His delight, you sense it. His celebration of life is so deep that you are not even able to feel it. He lived with a spiritual depth unknown before in human history. When you look into the depth of the heart of Jesus, you get dizzy, frightened. What an abyss! This real joy is beyond our understanding, attained only in the richest gifts of the Spirit. We understand suffering. We understand the language of sadness. It is easier to believe in a suffering Jesus – it reminds us of much that we are going through. But a laughing Jesus? Is that too much? Why can't we allow Jesus to laugh? Go in any church and look at Jesus. Sometimes, it is almost a caricature. He usually is painted long-faced, burdened, as sad as possible, almost neurotic. You would be afraid to be with such a person. There is no reason at all to see Jesus in such postures, except mirroring our own sadness and lack of living. The real Jesus is a bubbling spring, splashing cool water over all. At His touch, you become alive, green, living an ordinary life, but with more life in your life; you are filled with love, hope, and joy. The gospel is the "good news." Only bad news makes us gloomy and cynical. Good news is joyful and cheerful.

Jesus could not have been other than totally joyful. He was in unity with His Father. A sad-looking Jesus is utterly wrong, probably heretical, because it goes against the basic realization of Jesus Christ, fully human and fully divine. Someone who has attained the ultimate consciousness of life, who is at home in his Father's world, cannot be other than blissful and cheerful. Jesus must have had all the qualities of every flower, star, dance, song, and smile. He had come home. Why should He be long-faced! He was enjoying life!

If you want to understand Jesus, don't count only on how a painter pictures Him or what a minister says of Him because these have learned, speculated, philosophized, but they have not necessarily known Him. To know Jesus, you must un-cultivate your mind, cultivating instead the qualities of your heart. He is the innermost "no-thingness." He is "the way, and the truth, and the life" (John 14:6). He is joy. He is your joy and mine, here and now.

And would you think that Jesus never laughed? Impossible!

ℛ

4

Jesus Was Radical

It is difficult to deal with Jesus as a person. He is not an easy person to understand. You must be very cautious when you approach a furnace. You can approach a politician, a priest, a businessperson, anybody, without any great danger. But to approach Jesus is very, very difficult. You are approaching a fire. The closer you come, the more you will feel burned. Your masks disappear. Your lies disappear. Your rituals and your "religion" become secondary to His love.

Jesus is radical, so radical that he asks His followers to be "born again" (John 3:3-5), so radical that He makes all things new (Revelation 21:5; Ephesians 4:22-23). He doesn't ask to renew our institutions, laws, habits, or anything like that. He asks a complete rebirth of all ourselves: mind, heart, lifestyle, way of thinking. Everything about us is to be transformed. "You must lay aside your former way of life and the old self which deteriorates through illusion and desire, and acquire a fresh, spiritual way of thinking. You must put on that new man created in God's image, whose justice and holiness are born of truth" (Ephesians 4:22-24).

In other words, Jesus is disquieting. It is not convenient to meet with Him. He can shatter your life adjustments. He is "antisocial." He does not seem very "respectable." How could He be! He was a vagabond who didn't listen to those in His society. He was an extremist. He made friends with prostitutes, He ate with the wealthiest and the poorest, He made a mess in the temple, He took on the political and religious powers of His time, when He could have adjusted to the status quo and lived His life calmly, pacifically, and harmoniously. You feel uneasy before Him and you start trembling deep inside because He makes you feel that your life has been wasted thus far. He does not allow you the time and the convenience of dreaming and planning. For Him, there is no tomorrow. There is only now. So you have to change at this very minute. What a discomfort! You offer prayers and praise to Him because it is much easier to do so than to hear, "None of those who cry out, 'Lord, Lord,' will enter the Kingdom of God but only the one who does the will of my Father in heaven" (Matthew 7:21).

Prayers, praise, respect for the law make you a good person. You are then a conventional human being. You are a scholar. You are a "saint." But Jesus welcomed the company of the sinners and prostitutes without endorsing their misdeeds because these people loved life, even though in the wrong way, and life is passion. He wants them back to true life. Jesus had a passionate response to life. He loved life. He had an ardent appetite for being all that He could be. A zest for existence. Where there is a passion for life, there must be risks and possibilities to lose and to die. To live radically is not only to enjoy life, it is to live life with passion without calculating all the outcomes. To be radical is to love unconditionally, passionately, with all the risks to the human heart that this implies.

Only lovers can be really radical. Jesus was a radical lover. He extended his love to the poor, the rich, his friends, foreigners, strangers, "enemies," to everyone, and He freely laid down His life at the end in confirmation of His love. Real love expects you to risk everything and perhaps to die. That is why the company of Jesus is disturbing. You cannot be indifferent to Him. If you allow room for Him in your heart, you immediately become different. Jesus brings chaos. Everything inside you will be turned upside down. But out of this chaos, you will be born again, totally new. Jesus' first interest is not the social order as such. His main concern is human consciousness. When your innermost being is in order, society will take care of itself.

Christ was and will always be a sign of contradictions. "It is mercy I desire and not sacrifice, I have come to call, not the self-righteous, but sinners" (Matthew 9:13). Where usually are the best earthly goods? And where usually are the pain and suffering? Look around and see. Aren't very often the earthly goods in the possession of Christ's "enemies" and the suffering in the likes of His friends? Who are Jesus' friends? Aren't they the sinners in the first place! Didn't He place the pagan ways ahead of the traditional faithful ways! His community, the Jewish community, had excellent religious structures practices, rituals, preachers, chiefs, sacred books. But for Jesus, to possess good structures is something very different from living in faith and being saved. Of the pagan, for example, he said, "I tell you, I have never found so much faith among the Israelites" (Luke 7:9).

In religion, there is no professionalism. There are only amateurs. Jesus didn't find faith in the professional religious people of that time. In fact, the fiercest opposition to him came from the high priests and the religious people. These had long kept the faith, but in such a way that they didn't live it anymore. They had prayed for so long that they didn't pray with heart anymore. They had hoped for so long that they were not expecting anything to happen anymore.

Jesus, therefore, turned His face toward the pagans, the "heretics," the prostitutes, the sinners, the strangers, and the most simple people because these were waiting for something incredible. They hoped. They were open to Him. They were vulnerable. They had nothing to lose except their sinfulness. These people can recognize Jesus before the so-called righteous people. Their heads are not full of theologies, scriptures, opinions, traditions, laws. They know nothing. They are not programmed. They have a sense that their lives are futile – and are eager to convert. They are attracted to fire. But the so-called saints – leaders of churches and righteous people – are afraid of fire. They are afraid of hell, of God's punishment, of their own fears, of sinners, and, deep inside, of losing their positions and respectability.

To come close to Jesus, you need courage to risk and to lose. A sinner is qualified by an empty mind. For Jesus, the least is the greatest (Luke 9:48). Jesus accepted people as they were. Sinners were at ease with Him. He loved them, not their sins, but them. So the Pharisees complained to the disciples, "What reason can the Teacher have for eating with tax collectors and those who disregard the law?" (Matthew 9:11). Jesus seemed abnormal to them. He had to be unusual in their eyes. Jesus didn't behave as a "normal" individual in their society did. He didn't follow the ordinary rules. He didn't fit in, so to speak. He looked somehow eccentric. He didn't belong to their ordered society. He seemed the outsider. He seemed to come from some other planet. He was not realistic. He was not "real" in His words and actions. He must be proved wrong. Otherwise people would be wrong themselves. This was unacceptable.

Jesus seemed alone. Nobody seemed to understood Him. Who likes a person who is so different, so radical, so eager to change "our" religion and "our" ways? He seemed threatening. They crucified Him.

But Jesus was exceptionally aware. He accumulated knowledged intensity of awareness, not knowledge. You may have wealth, power, fame, commodities of the world, knowledge, philosophies, theories, ideologies, and the best of anything. Do these things really satisfy you? Only grace and love and awareness save you. "To the man who has, more will be given until he grows rich; the man who has not, will lose what little he has" (Matthew 13:12). This saying looks cruel, unkind, hard. We would have thought the opposite. Jesus said many "absurd" things like this. But awareness attracts more awareness and unawareness leads to less awareness. And all that you have accumulated melts away.

It is not easy to deal with a radical person like Jesus. At the same time, it is impossible to stay away from Him.

એ

5

Jesus Was a Rebel

Jesus failed as a "revolutionary." Jesus succeeded as a rebel.

On the day He was crucified, the crowd gathered to see whether or not He was going to perform a miracle. Nothing, it seemed, happened. He died as any other ordinary man dies – weak, surrendering, ridiculed.

A real rebel has to die this way because he refuses to use the means and the ways of extraordinary powers. Where a revolution fails, a rebellion usually succeeds.

Jesus' story is the story of weakness and human failure.

Jesus wasn't well-connected. He didn't have wealth, fame, respect, or anything that the world finds impressive. His resume seems so insignificant that nobody would be willing even to consider hiring Him. Plus, He lacked human connections totally. He was simple, so simple and free, so free that He became an inconvenience and a troublesomeness.

No, He didn't like His society as it was. How can Christ "like" any ordinary establishment! But He didn't blame society. A revolutionary would take care of that. But He was the rebel.

Jesus' rebellion was not political. He was not interested in power. His rebellion was not directed against anyone. But He was dissatisfied with any situation. He cared about both the victim and the ruler. He was not a "revolutionary." The moment a revolutionary takes possession of the destiny of people, he usually becomes archly antirevolutionary. A revolutionary, when the situation has changed, finds himself in the same situation that he just fought to overthrow.

Jesus' rebellion was of the Spirit. Wherever and whenever there was a barrier, Jesus would say no. He moved from society to the cosmos, and from social fiction to the universal realities. Real freedom was His noble goal. Nobody would be at ease with such a person. And if Jesus appeared on earth today, He would most likely have the same destiny! He would find Himself at odds with society and would end up on a similar cross. Every time a society – call it a church or anything else – becomes part of the establishment and settles down, it repeats what the rulers living in Jesus' time did for Him. A status quo is possible only without a Christ. Christ brought change. Change is life!

If Jesus came today, He would certainly destroy all that people have. He would be compassion. But who needs this? Weren't we raised for centuries in the tradition of believing in the violent, cruel, vengeful God that we can mollify by sacrifices and prayers and fasting and Sunday Mass? Weren't we supposed to imitate Him by becoming as vengeful as He was, through condemnations of sinners, excommunications, wars of religions, inquisitions, crusades? Jesus came to reveal that God was something else! He was an innocent, loving, compassionate, understanding God who would never cease to love us, in kindness.

Can we bear this? Are we willing, like Jesus, to make this shift in thinking, or do we rather prefer the old security, crucifying Him and all that He revealed?

Jesus, in fact, can be the destroyer of your selfish, worldly dreams, especially the dearest ones in which you have been investing so much money and/or time.

The very moment Jesus appears in society, the whole society will be shaken, like an earthquake. The fundamental question explodes in your mind: Who is right, me or Jesus? All my "havings" or His "being"? Jesus was murdered in Jerusalem. He can be murdered again in Washington, Paris, London, Belfast, Beirut, or the Vatican, and in you-him-her-me. Two thousand years ago, people followed Jesus to a certain extent. But deep down, they felt that He was leading them beyond human comprehension and they became afraid. They had to kill Him to escape the chaos. Aren't we ready to do the same, today?

It would be a very sad day if Jesus came and nobody bothered to stone Him. Jesus hurts. He provokes. He challenges. He leads you to unknown places in yourself. He is interested in changing your heart, in making of you a new person. He puts things upside down, and you are scared.

With Jesus, you cannot be indifferent. You love Him or you crucify Him. Even today. When He was murdered some two thousand years ago, it was only the beginning. You cannot be indifferent with such a man as Jesus. You have to do something about Him. He can never be a commodity that is bought and sold, though some "Christians" have invented and decorated a Jesus for the market. You can be a "Christian" for convenience. You can even make money from it. But you can never be a real Christian just for convenience. If you really are one of His followers, you have to expect troubles. You cannot expect to be on your throne, when Jesus Himself ended on the cross. Jesus reminds His disciples, "If you find that the world hates you, know it has hated me before you . . . no slave is greater than his master. They will harry you as they harried me" (John 15:18, 20).

Your transformation will happen when you adjust yourself to living in Christ, not the other way around.

If you consider Jesus as a decoration only, or part of a certain collection, you don't really relate to Him. Christianity, in a sense, has nothing to do with Christ. Christ is rebellion. If you want to understand Christ, you have to go beyond Christianity. The original intuition of Christ has to be sought beyond all the limitations of institutions and beyond all the alterations that were imposed throughout the centuries that followed His death until now.

Christ is not a decoration on the wall or on your chest. Christ is that "something" that makes you the "salt of the earth" (Matthew 5:13), the "light of the world" (Matthew 5:14), and the little yeast that leavens the entire dough (Matthew 13:33; Luke 13:21; 1 I Corinthians 5:6; Galatians 5:9).

You cannot find a compromise with such a rebel. You join Him in living a life of real love.

಄

6

Catalysis

Jesus loved people. He never missed an opportunity to make contact with them. He did not place restrictions on them. He always was ready to sit down with them, even at the well, where He met the Samaritan woman who said, "You are a Jew. How can you ask me, a Samaritan and a woman, for a drink?" (John 4:9). Even in the Pharisee's home: "Jesus went to the Pharisee's home and reclined to eat" (Luke 7:36).

Why did Jesus do such unusual and "strange" things in His time? What were His secrets and methods and motives?

Jesus' way was His radiating presence.

Jesus wanted people to be in contact with Him. He wanted them to be in His loving presence. The very loving presence of Jesus produced love. People were transformed by His touch, by His being with them, by His loving presence. He was a catalytic agent.

In Jesus' presence, something ought to happen. His very presence provokes you, inspires you, changes you. In His presence, you can't stay the same. Something will start happening in you.

Hydrogen and oxygen, in the presence of electricity, become water. "Something" different in a new substance astounds us.

Jesus was not a doctor, or a scientist, or a scholar, or a philosopher. He was not even a theologian. He was a healer. When He saw the paralyzed man, He said, "Your sins are forgiven" (Matthew 9:2). He did not say, "Rise and walk." A good doctor would have tried to put the man on his feet. Jesus looked further. He knew that a cure can often be a result of a healed life.

Jesus' words were alive; they seemed to have miraculous effects. They were the words understood by common people, the hard-working farmers, the diligent gardeners, the eager fishermen, the woodcutters, the beggars, the prostitutes, the gamblers, the drunkards, but they were always full of His divine presence. They were always spoken from His heart to the hearts of others. They were impressive. Just being there, someone will be awakened. It is so intriguing to see this kind of miraculous action without action. Jesus, very often, did not do anything. He, very often, did not intervene directly. But the radiation of His vital presence changed the situation He was in. In His presence, someone would wake up, would have a different look at existence with the same eyes but a changed heart. At His touch, an ordinary, poor, uncultured, uneducated fisherman evolved into an enlightened person, a tax collector became an apostle, a prostitute became a pure woman, the plain water was changed into wine. "They (Simon and Andrew) immediately abandoned their nets and became his followers" (Matthew 4:20). "She (a sinner) brought in a vase of perfumed oil and stood behind him at his feet, weeping so that her tears fell upon his feet" (Luke 7:37-38). This may be the best way to meet Jesus; from "behind," "weeping" as wounded human beings. The meeting with Jesus is not a meeting of the heads, but of the hearts. "Righteous" people do not come to Jesus. They want Him to come Himself to them. They are proud of their knowledge and "good" behavior. Someone who really wants to come and is very curious to see what is going on comes in the dark. Professor Nicodemus came when everybody had left, otherwise his knowledge would be suspect. A person of knowledge cannot understand Jesus. He can discuss Scripture, prove something, or play with words. But Jesus is the Word that became flesh. So knowledge alone is a poor method when it comes to dealing with Jesus. Something much more profound is required.

Jesus did not use some eccentric techniques. The real attraction is His extraordinary presence, His spiritual magnetism. It was not a question of physical beauty, genius, a high position, prestige, wealth, or fame. No! It was just His being there. In His presence, something you cannot really define with words happened. Something mysterious, ineffable, extraordinary filled their hearts. His presence was electrifying. There is no greater alchemist than Jesus.

Wherever, whenever Jesus blossoms, all existence blossoms and becomes blessed. Jesus' presence changes the quality of relationships because He transforms the quality of one's consciousness. One's thinking becomes different, as well as one's way of feeling, seeing, touching, tasting, and behaving.

Those who were and are in the presence of Jesus – who breathe Him, drink Him, eat Him, allow Him to enter into their innermost shrines – cannot stay the same. Jesus is so alive, so living, so contagious, so dangerous, and so passionate that He transforms everyone and everything He touches. His presence makes miracles. United with Christ, you are another Christ. You are His miracle.

℘

7

Is Jesus Bringing Chaos to the World?

Jesus was a person who brought disorder, confusion, and chaos into the society of Moses. And He posed a threat to the power of Rome.

What do you expect from someone like Jesus? He simply was true to Himself, to His Father's will, and to His own mission. When you are true to yourself, you are going to feel the hypocrisy of the world surging against you. Jesus felt strongly how false, phony, hypocritical, possessive, jealous, and power hungry were the people in the society in which he lived. He didn't soften His feelings about these people. He reacted to them with the force of the truth. What was established was now shaking to its very foundation. He was about to become the new cornerstone.

A good, ordinary citizen usually lives the present through the past. He learns his country's history. He knows its laws. He enjoys what is already established, already grounded. He has an investment, so to speak, in its past. And if someone like Jesus comes and says, "You were told, but I tell you," you are not going to accept it. Think about it. Was it not normal that Jesus wasn't immediately accepted

26

by His own people? He was born a Jew, but the Jews did not accept Him.

Jesus didn't follow the social rules. When He met with that woman of Samaria, He broke a social rule. When He was a guest of Zacchaeus, He scandalized everybody in the street. When He enjoyed Himself at parties, He was suspected of overindulging in food and drink. When He healed people on the Sabbath, He didn't carry out the letter of the law. When He talked to the sinner, He was suspected of not being on the side of right conduct. So the fear of the guardians of the laws was quite normal. These people were responsible to defend the discipline of the temple, their own inspired religion, the structure of their society built on prophets. Jesus was a danger to the order. When they became aware of this danger, they realized that what constituted security and comfort for them was going to be shaken – it could collapse. Their safety walls were shaken. They were not going to enjoy "peace" anymore. Something was moving. Even the ordinary people, people of the street, were feeling this surge. When, for example, they cried out: "Hosanna! Blessed is he who comes in the name of the Lord"(Mark 11:9). What, in reality, motivated their enthusiasm? Was this for the prophet of Galilee? Was it for the preacher of the Kingdom of God? Was He the Messiah who was going to liberate them from the Romans? Perhaps. However, most of all, the people of the streets were feeling that, with this man of Palestine, their world was changing in the capital.

But who and what really was changing?

Jesus wasn't interested in taking over the material world to bring a new regime. He wasn't even interested in bringing a new materialistic society. His message was to bring a new human consciousness, a new heart, and a new spiritual order arising in the innermost being. Jesus brought chaos. He knew that when the periphery is in disorder, one seeks to go within. When there is anarchy outside, you look for your real home inside, and you come to your own center. When everything is fine outside, who bothers to seek inside? Perhaps a new life is especially possible when outer chaos succeeds. For the existing order, Jesus was the most dangerous man ever to exist. His presence is like a Spirit alarm. He wants to awaken the you in you. He puts things upside down. He has "funny" ideas, unorthodox. He disturbs your "beautiful" dreams. But, somehow, you feel attracted to Him. He is an extraordinary magnet. He is appealing to you because He appeals to your soul's depth. With Him, it is an involved relationship. Hence the excitement and the fear. You may choose, like the Jews, to kill him, to defend your own periphery against your center, or to defend the man-made order against the God-made one.

The Jews were defending the law of Moses. Jesus was talking about that powerful energy called *love*. Moses, in a sense, brought civilization. He brought the laws. That society cannot exist without Moses. Those laws were the very foundation of that society. But Jesus brought love. And love is beyond and above law. Law is a must. But it is not enough. Without love, is life worth living? Jesus brought something from the eternal into the known world. He added love's meanings to the rules of everyday life. Moses makes you a good citizen, the "right" individual, the respected individual, the person who is on the right track. Jesus didn't care about "respectability." He wanted to reach out. He spoke with a prostitute. He moved with sinners, drunkards, sick people. He was like a river flowing free, making everything green around it.

You can easily believe Moses. You follow the Ten Commandments and all the other Jewish rules. You know when you are right or wrong. With Jesus, it is not so. On the surface, you don't even know if you are right or wrong. He would tell you to accept and not to judge, that He has come to fulfill, not to destroy. Then He would say, "It was said, but I tell you . . ." Jesus brought "confusion and conflict" – a new awareness – to people's minds. He did not follow the rules of logic. He did not accept the standards of His time. He refused a place of power. For Him, power resided in serving: "Whoever wants to rank first among you must serve the needs of all" (Mark 10:44). He bought no home. He preferred the lilies of the field to social privileges. He praised the poor, not the rich. He preached mercy before sacrifice. He felt freedom in going beyond the conventional values of either the Judaic or the Roman systems. He created great chaos, the necessary condition for His condemnation. His assassination was a political-sociological-psychological-religious act. It seemed absolutely logical. Who can bear such a pure love as Jesus'! His presence is threatening. Somehow people feel much more secure with laws than with love. Real love is always associated with death. When you kill Jesus, you kill your innermost, your deepest center in favor of your periphery. Jesus is a divine fire. He was always on the side of the person against the claims of the legalistic religion. He emphasized the priority of human values over conventionally "religious" ones. "The sabbath was made for man, not man for the sabbath" (Mark 2:27). That is why the gospel's call transcends any social structure. The person of faith does not only interpret history, he changes it. In this sense, all social structures will remain subject to evolution as long as human life lasts.

Did Jesus create a chaos? Yes – He created a new world order. His ideas were not organized according to our logic. He turned the world upside down with His divine love. He expects your love to do the same. Be Christ today in your world!

ဆ

8

About the Logic of Jesus

Jesus was not a professor of logic. He was not a doctrinarian of any sort. He did not have a Ph.D. He did not have a philosophical system. He did not institutionalize anything. He did not invent any rite. He knew nothing about Aristotle's logic. He did not write, not even a single word. And yet, He taught the truth. He taught it in a very special way – in paradoxes. With Him, you hear what you do not expect to hear. His truth astonishes and scandalizes. He does not care about a coherent logic, nor about an intellectual understanding. He does not even care about being understood. He works at another level, with a lot of surprises. He wants people to trust Him. To understand and to be convinced are matters of intelligence and reason, therefore irrelevant for a work of transformation. To be transformed, one needs to be touched. One needs a flame. One needs a heart.

What is more important, in Jesus' point of view, is something discrete, small, poetic. A flash of light. The little story, a parable, a paradox, speak to you and remain in your soul's depths more than any scholarly treatise. You may understand a treatise clearly. But you can never fully understand a parable. There is a challenge in it. In it, two and two do not necessarily make four. The prodigal son is more loved than his brother. The worker of the eleventh hour is paid as much as the one who worked all day long. The rich one is unhappy. One must leave the ninety-nine sheep and go after the one that is lost. The first ones will be the last ones. Happy are those who are persecuted for justice, those who are crying. He who wants to gain his life will have to lose it, and so on.

What kind of logic is this?!

The secret of a parabolic and paradoxical method, you see, is the imperceptible transference of values. Jesus puts you on a love level that you did not expect.

He may take and demand distances:

Why did you search for me? Did you not know I had to be in my Father's house? (Luke 2:49)

If anyone comes to me without turning his back on his father and mother, his wife and his children, his brothers and sisters, indeed his very self, he cannot be my follower. (Luke 14:26)

My mission is to spread, not peace, but division. I have come to set a man at odds with his father, a daughter with her mother, a daughter-in-law with her mother-in-law. (Matthew 10:34-35)

My mother and my brothers are those who hear the word of God and act upon it. (Luke 8:21)

He may put things upside down:

Blest are the poor in spirit. . . . Blest are the sorrowing. . . . Blest are the lowly. . . . Blest are those persecuted for holiness' sake. . . . Blest are you when they insult you and persecute you and utter every kind of slander against you because of me. (Matthew 5:3-11)

Jesus said that in the midst of Jewish and Roman people who were known for their full support of the rich and the strong. For them, power and wealth were signs of divine preference (remember Job's story). What was considered wisdom and security becomes, with Jesus, danger and foolishness. The man who had a good harvest heard these stinging words:

> You fool! This very night your life shall be required of you. To whom will all this piled-up wealth of yours go? That is the way it works with the man who grows rich for himself instead of growing rich in the sight of God. (Luke 12:20-21)

And elsewhere Jesus said:

> It is easier for a camel to pass through a needle's eye than for a rich man to enter the Kingdom of God. (Mark 10:25)

Jesus may also use harsh words to shock and condemn. To the Pharisees, He said:

> I assure you that tax collectors and prostitutes are entering the Kingdom of God before you. (Matthew 21:31)

> Woe to you scribes and pharisees, you frauds! (Matthew 23:13)

And when they threw the woman caught in adultery in front Him, and told Him, "In the law, Moses ordered such women to be stoned. What do you have to say about the case?" (John 8:5), Jesus kept silent, at first. Then He passed from legalism to psychoanalysis and said to them, "Let the man among you who has no sin be the first to cast a stone at her" (John 8:7). Jesus' opponents always wanted to discuss things on a legal, theoretical, and general level. Jesus wanted to put things on a personal level. Look at yourself. Examine your own conscience. Behave yourself. Heart is more important than mind. When people consulted Him about the essential in law, He devalorized severely the religious observances, and He put compassion ahead of sacrifices and holocausts (Matthew 9:13, 12:7; Mark 12:33). What Jesus did not stand for was self-satisfaction and self-sufficiency. He did not want a self-made salvation. He did not want ceremonies replacing authentic adoration. He did not want legalism replacing moral truth. He did not want virtue, alms, fasting, or even prayer as warranty certificates for His Kingdom. What He really wanted was for His followers to pass to another level, to a "within" religion. When Jesus healed the sick, He addressed, first of all and especially, the guilt involved (Mark 5:34-36; 9:23; 10:52; 11:24; Matthew 9:29; 8:13; Luke 7:50; 17:19; 18:42). To the centurion He said, "Go home. It shall be done because you trusted" (Matthew 8:13). To Simon, His host, He said, "You see this woman? I came to your home and you provided me with no water for my feet. . . . her many sins are forgiven – because of her great love" (Luke 7:44-47). To Martha He said, "Martha, Martha, you are anxious and upset about many things; one thing only is required. Mary has chosen the better portion and she shall not be deprived of it" (Luke 10:41-42).

Jesus was not an acetic, as John the Baptizer was. He was even accused of eating and drinking to a certain excess. But no one accused Him, however, of not being a man of prayer. He prayed all the time, everywhere. He prayed not only to teach us a lesson or because this is something that has to be done, after all. Jesus prayed because He believed. He prayed because His Father wanted trust, His family needed openness, His friends needed presence, His enemies needed love, His life needed meaning and purpose.

To found His church, He didn't go to doctors, to scholars, or to some intellectual elite. He chose, rather, ignorant people. And to His disciples who were those simple men, He said, "You are the light of the world" (Matthew 5:14). No system was necessary. No official documents. No sophisticated constitutions. No colossal arguments. No infinite number of books of interpretations and speculations. He was "the way, and the truth, and the life" (John 14:6). That simple. Period.

Aristotle was more logical. And how much easier he really was! With him, two and two always make four. At this level of logic, you cannot have another answer. But with Jesus, you have to proceed from one level to another, from what you understand to what you may believe. A perfect speculation is far away. Only the paradoxes of parables are human. Only God can be the perfect human being, and He was. Aristotle and other philosophers have helped to deliver the logic existing in the human mind. Jesus went much more deeply. He liberated the human being. He generated the human being to his or her genuine nature, which the human being cannot do on his or her own. He made the divine human and the human divine. He identified the second commandment with the first and suggested that the way we deal with our neighbor is the very way we deal with God. This is beyond our normal comprehension, indeed. How impossible sometimes!

Jesus lacked "normal" logic. He lived love.

℘

9

The Eye of the Heart

The heart holds the key to God. The head can never understand God. Only the heart does.

God does not come as a syllogism, a thought, a speculation, an ideology, a doctrine. God comes as a song, a feeling, a tear, a laughter, love. The word "God" is not God. You may have the best theories on it. If it remains an abstraction for you, you are an atheist.

The only language that God understands is the language of the heart: love. People try to communicate with God in many languages — Latin, Greek, Arabic, French, English, German, Chinese, the language of theology, the language of philosophy, the language of science, the language of the Bible. Nothing will do. God is not interested in any language that the head knows. His only interest is his own language — love.

To the head, the heart seems childish and illogical. To the heart, the head seems useless and superficial. You really understand and really know when you feel. Otherwise you keep thinking and thinking and thinking, but you never know. With your head, you ask questions and questions and questions. With your heart, you long for love and love and love. When you fix your head on something, you may find a temporary answer. When you fix your heart on something, a miracle will happen, and you will have the answer. The head can give you an answer already known. Only the heart cries "eureka!"

In this world, the head certainly leads to success. Reason runs this world. With your heart, you can be a failure. Since you don't exploit, you don't fit in. You don't lie. You don't use facades and masks. You don't bargain. You feel yourself far from the profit mentality. You are a stranger in the midst of the crowd. You may feel secluded. Alone.

In the marketplace, who needs the heart? Who needs poetry, emotions, sensitivity, compassion? The heart cannot purchase any commodities of itself. The heart knows nothing about competition, calculation, and hostility. It knows nothing about ideologies and their games, abstractions and their generalities, concepts and their unrealities. The laws of the market are not the laws of the heart, and when they seem to be using the heart, they do it to make a profit, not out of caring. In the market, who cares?

Matters of the heart are subtle. You feel, you cry, you laugh, you dance, you weep, you shout – and you do all this from the heart. And slowly you feel a change coming, a transformation. Then new values arise. Those of the head become secondary. You appear crazy. Only crazy people move along the path of the heart. Only with the eyes of the heart can you see reality. You touch reality. You live reality. The head is no more the controller. It is no more the boss. And you realize how pretentious the head was by creating ideas about the real and never grasping it. What is worse, we keep investing in the head rather than in the heart. Our culture, our schools, and our universities are of and for the head. The head has become too heavy, and the heart goes on shrinking. The heart is neglected, ignored. We are violent, savage, unloving. We have lost the true taste of enjoying the wholeness of life. We no longer take time to explore all our dimensions. We miss the best. The head adds tension. Only the heart knows how to enjoy.

When we look at someone, we often look in a superficial way. We never look into anyone's heart because if we do, we become insecure, involved, vulnerable, and we cannot remain self-centered, mean, and unkind. It is dangerous to look at someone's heart. We will be touched by love and filled by the higher values. Our priorities will change. We will change. With the head it is safer. We may stay aloof, far away, false. On the surface we may appear very kind and loving, but deep down much hatred is there. When we learn to penetrate each other's heart, we become authentic and genuine; many of our masks will be stripped away.

Our "personality" works against us. It is a barrier for the communications of the heart. Society compels us to live with unreal faces. Only when we discard them will we be able to penetrate the kingdom of the heart. And only at that moment we will have a foretaste of the divine because the divine is available to those who have become capable of knowing the reality of the human heart. And at that moment we can really pray. Prayer is the language of the heart. Prayer is unscientific and has nothing to do with the head. Prayer is a matter of the heart like every divine thing. A person in prayer cannot prove anything because, for the heart the conclusion comes first.

The great revolution in human life is the *metanoia* – repentance, conversion, change of the heart. It is a radical change. "I will give you a new heart and place a new spirit in you, taking from your bodies your stony hearts and giving you natural hearts" (Ezekiel 36:26). "Change your hearts, for the kingdom of heaven is at hand" (Matthew 3:2). The changed heart brings a tremendous revolution in the personality, a conversion. One changes values and grows in love without restrictions. And one becomes pure. Only the pure of heart will see God (Matthew 5:8). And this is what enlightenment is all about: the awakening of the third eye, the eye of the heart.

Only the eye of the heart makes things real.

Only the eye of the heart allows you to grow.

Our interpretations of the Scriptures and all our logical structures may actually betray the truth. The divine mystery is revealed only in the depths of the human heart.

ॐ

1 0

The Dynamics of the Kingdom of God

The announcement of the Kingdom of God is at the center of Jesus' message. God's reign is already here, and it is yet to come.

When the Pharisees asked Jesus when the Kingdom of God was to come, he answered, "The reign of God is already in your midst" (Luke 17:21). The kingdom has begun.

This Kingdom is impossible to see because it is not a noun. It is a verb. It is in action. When? Now. Where? "In your midst." Jesus sees the Kingdom at work in the interdependence, in the amongness, and in the horizontal – as well as the vertical – consciousness.

The wealthy, who are very much object oriented, cannot see where the Kingdom is. That is why it is so difficult for the rich to enter the Kingdom.

In the amongness, there are special dynamics. Jesus says, "To what shall I compare the reign of God? It is like yeast which a woman took to knead into three measures of flour until the whole mass of dough began to rise" (Luke 13:21). The dough becomes leavened throughout by the yeast. Amongness has this dynamic characteristic of trans-formation.

Jesus never talked about the Kingdom as a separate life or as a withdrawal from the ordinary life. He prayed, "I do not ask you to take them out of the world. . . . As you have sent me into the world, so I have sent them into the world" (John 17:15, 18). The life of which Jesus speaks is a life available to everyone. It is the everyday life, all the activities that men and women share everywhere all the time. The Kingdom is on earth. "Your will be done on earth as it is in heaven" (Matthew 6:10). "The field is the world, the good seed the citizens of the Kingdom" (Matthew 13:38). And this is also eternal life; for eternal life begins here below. From the past, you usually move on to the future. In the present, somehow you become still and you go deeper and deeper into more present. In the present, you lose the notion of time. When you move vertically – up and down, toward the height or toward the depth – you live in eternity, not in time. You live the everlasting life. Jesus said, "You cannot tell by careful watching when the reign of God will come. Neither is it a matter of reporting that it is 'here' or 'there'" (Luke 17:20-21). The Kingdom of God is eternal. It is always here, "already in your midst" (Luke 17:21). To understand this, you must put away the notion of time that moves from the past to the future along a straight line. Jesus was talking about depth and full awareness, not about what we call time. That is why He can say, "Eternal life is this: to know you, the only true God, and him whom you have sent, Jesus Christ" (John 17:3), and "Whoever has seen me has seen the Father" (John 14:9). You transcend time and space. You do not know about God. You know God. This knowing has more from being than from knowl-edge.

The Kingdom of God has the mode of being in the first place. Being has a profound existential energy. Being the mustard seed or being the yeast, as the parables describe them, is a very dynamic image of the Kingdom. The weakest and most insignificant seed becomes the greatest tree. The whole dough leavens and rises by the yeast. This is not a question of faith only. It is a reality you can touch and see growing. In fact, the coming of the Kingdom is made possible and "realized" in proportion to how much the disciples of Christ live the life of the Kingdom in the circumstances of their own time and place – How much they live existentially their love of God, their openness, their simplicity, and their "beatitudes." By their example of a truly Christian understanding of the world, which is incarnated in an active application of their faith to the problems of their time, they show the love of Christ for men: "This is how all will know you for my disciples: your love for one another" (John 13:35). "I pray that they may be [one] in us, that the world may believe that you sent me" (John 17:21). And by that fact, they make Him visibly present in the world, and they let Him grow and grow as the tree and the yeast of the parables.

But to be able to do that, and consequently to be qualified for citizenship in the Kingdom of God, the disciples of Christ cannot count on themselves, but on the Holy Spirit who dwells and works within them in a way that their lives become a continuous and progressive conversion and transformation. And by this, they transform others and allow themselves to be transformed by and with others, in Christ. The Kingdom of God, which is liberation, is built by the Holy Spirit working through the efforts of those whose thirst for justice drives them to build a more human world. The Kingdom of God is where chains are broken and barriers of selfishness are destroyed. The Kingdom of God belongs to those who struggle and fight for love, justice, and peace. It is in the profane that the Kingdom of God will penetrate and work and leaven and grow. The profane is the field for the coming of the Kingdom of God. The Kingdom of God will completely penetrate the whole of creation, which becomes transparent, so transparent that you can touch the divine in it.

In this state of becoming, there is a lot of energy, a lot of dynamic transformation, a real revolution – not a political revolution, but the revolution of the Spirit. Jesus was not interested in changing the society per se, like the politicians. He was interested in changing hearts. His path is the path of the heart. When the heart changes, society is bound to change at the same time. Jesus wants his disciple to move within-ward first, not east or west, not north or south, but in depth, to the very heart, God-ward. When the heart is illuminated by the Holy Spirit, we reform our lives: "This is the time of fulfillment. The reign of God is at hand! Reform your lives and believe in the gospel" (Mark 1:15). Then the world outside will start to talk the language of the Spirit. Innocence, purification, emptiness, vulnerability, surrendering, receptivity, poverty of the spirit are the first requirements to let God work. Calculation, cleverness, cunning, accumulation of riches are useless in the Kingdom of God. "How hard it is for the rich to enter the Kingdom of God!" (Mark 10:23). To the individual who accumulates things to prove his or her self-worth through possessions, the door of the Kingdom of God will be closed. Visible wealth can make you somebody in the world, but it can never fulfill you. Only "nobodies" – people who put all selfishness aside – are qualified for the Kingdom of God, since they trust the Holy Spirit to work, not their wealth.

Yes, the world must be transformed. But not through a political revolution, which is usually a search for power and personal interest, and therefore temporary, phony, and banal. The only worthwhile revolution is the one that starts within and expands in the amongness. This is the strategy of the Holy Spirit. Allow the Holy Spirit to come. "No one can see the reign of God unless he is begotten from above" (John 3:3). Then you will "not be afraid" to "go and carry the news to my brothers" (Matthew 28:10; John 20:17).

"The reign of God is already in your midst" (Luke 17:21). Love, the dynamic of the Kingdom of God, makes things real.

11

Which Sin Was Worse?

In the Gospel according to Luke (15:11-32), there is the famous parable of the prodigal son. This parable is mysterious, puzzling, and especially "unfair."

Here is the younger son, who is roguish and mischievous – a pleasure-seeking spendthrift who seems irresponsible – and has no interest in remaining loyal to his family or his tradition.

And here is the older son, who is dutiful, hardworking, patient, moral, righteous, loyal, and virtuous.

Which son was right? The pleasure-seeking one or the responsible one? The immediate and seemingly obvious answer would of course give credit to the latter. But the Kingdom of God has a different answer. When the father saw the younger son coming back, he "threw his arms around his neck and kissed him." Then he said to his servants, "Quick! Bring out the finest robe and put it on him. Take the fatted calf and kill it. Let us eat and celebrate."

Unfair! Unfair! Unfair! The father is rewarding the sinner and ignoring the responsible and dutiful son. What is going on here? The logic of God is different from our logic. In the context of the Kingdom of God, our logic does not seem to be of any importance.

The point of this parable is that a sin against love is much worse than any other sin. The sin of the spirit is far more grave than the sin of the body. In fact, no form of vice – whether worldliness, drunkenness, lust, greed – does more to paganize society than evil temper. Look at the older son and give him credit for all his virtues. But take a closer look at this man who is standing outside his father's door. He "grew angry" and "would not go in." Don't you see embodied in that angry person the elements of the loveless soul (jealousy, pride, uncharitableness, cruelty, self-righteousness, touchiness, doggedness, sulkiness)? Don't you think it is worse for us to adopt (and for others to live with!) such a disposition than to be overly concerned about sins of the body? Jesus made it clear when he said, "I assure you that tax collectors and prostitutes are entering the Kingdom of God before you" (Matthew 21:31). A person with such a temper could make heaven miserable for everyone there.

Attitude is very significant. The older son "would not go in," showing what was going on within him. The celebration at the return of his brother was a test of his love, a revelation of his unloving nature, an opportunity to demonstrate that his loyalty and hard work constituted a mask that served the purpose of hiding a certain rottenness beneath. But he was not sincere. "For years now I have slaved for you. I never disobeyed one of your orders, yet you never gave me so much as a kid goat to celebrate with my friends. Then, when this son of yours returns after having gone through your property with loose women, you killed the fatted calf for him."

Do you see the logic we humans use? We calculate our acts. We do things with the expectation of getting something in return. Even heaven becomes a bargain. We pray, fast, offer sacrifices in order to accumulate more points in heaven. Wrong! If the younger son did something wrong, the older one did no better. The sin of the heart and spirit is much more serious than the sin of the body. Hence it is not enough to deal with what is right or wrong in the conduct of the body, or with a structure, a law, or an institution. We must go to the source that makes things happen and effect change there. Only then would the unloving attitude of the older son and the frivolousness of the younger son have no reason to develop in the first place. Fortunately, the two of them have the same forgiving Father. God is always ready to forgive, even before you ask forgiveness: "While he (the younger son) was still a long way off, his father caught sight of him and was deeply moved. He ran out to meet him." And "but his (the older son's) father came out and began to plead with him." The forgiveness of the father is the act that reconciles the two brothers in a common celebration. A purification of two wrongdoings: pleasureseeking and refusal to accept others and share their joy; the miracle of God's forgiveness; the miracle of God's love!

We can take these two brothers as different aspects of our own persons. One part of us may identify with the older brother – the part that likes to be ruled by a strong sense of duty, has an ardent desire to conform and to please, and has a legitimate need to appear righteous. Another part of us – the joy of life, the spontaneity and the vulnerability demonstrated by the younger brother – would be driven into our subconscious to become our enemy. At times, however, we may choose to identify with the headstrong brother, pushing our responsible and serious side into the subconscious. So we will have going on within us a kind of "civil war," with a lot of repressions, obsessions, and suffering. If we become too self-righteous, we become terribly demanding and we may lose the joy of living. But if we indulge in pleasure to an inordinate degree, our pleasure will never be complete, will never be satisfied, because it will always be lacking something that we cannot define. The competition between these two aspects of our being should result in wholeness. The qualities of the one should complement the shortcomings of the other; the two "brothers" will achieve mutual acceptance and reconciliation. And only at that time will the older-brother aspect will live with the humor, joy, and spontaneity of the younger brother, and the younger-brother aspect live with the maturity and conscience of the older brother. And this was what the father was trying to bring about. He welcomed back the younger son because this one had "come to his senses," and he invited the older son to self-confrontation and to recognition of the truth: "My son, you are with me always, and everything I have is yours. But we had to celebrate and rejoice! This brother of yours was dead, and has come back to life. He was lost, and is found."

The Kingdom of God does not operate by our rules and logic. Rather, the Kingdom of God demands forgiveness, reconciliation, wholeness, and unity in love.

ॐ

1 2

How Can a Man Be Born Again?

How can a man be born again? (John 3:4). Every person, every generation, every civilization has tried to answer Nicodemus's question – through a new ideology, a new political system, a new philosophy of life, a new lifestyle, a new ethical understanding, a new behavior, a new technology, a new experience, a new drug, a new pleasure. Each new "right" answer was identified with a given social, political, economic, psychological, or even religious structure. But Christ's answer was, "No one can see the reign of God unless he is begotten from above" (John 3:3). People, except by God's grace, look in the wrong direction.

To be born again is not a certain adjustment to social and religious requirements. It is not a certain change in our moral resolutions. It is not a kind of strict self-discipline. It is not finding ways to gain more respect, maybe through a high post of responsibility. It is not longing for a new life because the old familiar one reached a dead end. It is not some kind of emotional conversion followed by a certain change in rituals, attitudes, convictions, or a new set of activities or religious practices. All these ordinary answers are not sufficient to meet Christ's demand.

The rebirth of which Christ is speaking, which is a "new creation" in and by the Spirit, is not a simple event. It is a continuous and dynamic renewal within. It is a continuous growth in the life of the Spirit. It is that transparence that allows love to shine by itself in the new creation. It ultimately lies in allowing God to do with us whatever He is pleased to do. It is a new identity altogether. It is a divine birth. That is why it is worthwhile to risk everything in order to be born again, not in the flesh, but in God.

To be born again, however, does not mean to become somebody else or to become another person different from who or what you are. To be born again means to become your own self. To become yourself, you must die to self. You must allow your false self to die and your true self to come forward. When your outer self becomes secondary, your inner self will surface. You will feel born again.

To be born again is a psychological and, above all, a spiritual process. If you can be one with the universe, the whole universe becomes a mother. If you don't separate yourself from the cosmos, you are in the womb again. In this communion, God reveals His plans to you. You become a new creature. "See, I make all things new!" (Revelation 21:5). You are born again.

To be born again is to be awakened. An awakened person is innocent. He does not have prejudices. He does not judge others. If life is lived with alertness, joy, silence, and deep understanding, one does not grow old; one rather grows young while growing up. Growing old is a physical process. Growing up and growing young are spiritual processes. Your being cannot grow old, but it can remain immature. To be born again is to let your true being grow up, higher and higher. The higher the aim, the younger the muscles will be. The higher the spiritual goal, the younger the true self will be. Awakening does not follow the rules of physical aging.

To be born again is to have access to another living state of reality, another state of consciousness, another level of being. It is not a question of transformation only; it is rather abandoning one milieu to another. This world in which we live, with all its imperfections and miseries, while remaining in a sense the same, has become a completely different world, precisely because we now have new eyes. When we are born again, our enemies become our friends through forgiveness, our sickness becomes an opportunity for spiritual growth, and our economic difficulties become secondary issues, because we know that there is Someone above who looks after even the birds of the sky. All our confusions and frustrations and depressions and worries will collapse instantly because they are wasting time and energy. Rebirth rather than transformation. In transformation, there is something left from the old self. In rebirth, nothing remains the same and yet everything is the same. Our new state of consciousness creates a completely new reality, a new self, and that is why a new reality is born.

Being born again trails a long history behind it. In this sense, it is an achievement. But being born again is always the beginning of a new spiritual life. In this sense, it is a continuous renewal. But above all, being born again is a gift from God, which is much more important than the physical birth. We must accept this gift. We must choose to be born again.

ॐ

13

The Gospel According to Children

Jesus said, "I assure you, unless you change and become like little children you will not enter the Kingdom of God" (Matthew 18:2).

So, being like children is the requirement for entering the Kingdom of God. It is a must, otherwise the door of the Kingdom of God is closed.

But what does it mean to be like children? A child has a consciousness filled with wonder and freshness. A child hears and sees things as if for the first time. Every day the sun rises for the child. A child admires the beauty of the sun without comparing it with how it was the day before.

A child is innocent, direct, natural, and spontaneous. He does not calculate with ulterior motives. She is not clever, not cunning. She trusts. She is a child. She lets things happen. She is simple. She just opens herself up to life. She listens, sees, tastes, smells, touches, laughs, cries, and sings. She notices a butterfly on the wing, a river flowing, a bird singing, a rainbow. These throw her into a state of exaltation. She has no speculative answers. She does not need them. And yet her answers are always there.

A child has no "name" yet, no identity, no limitations. He is potentiality, one with existence. He is not limited, has no prejudices, doesn't disguise definitions and expectations. A child simply is. He is vast. He does not have a formed character yet. A character defines, limits, puts on armor, "kills," drives you crazy. A child, in growing, learns to survive. He learns to be mad, to lie, to not be himself. He learns to be conditioned, to "destroy" his true authenticity and his own sincerity. He learns to compromise.

A child does not know, therefore she cannot sin. A child lives the life of spontaneity. Not that knowledge is bad by itself, but it is through knowledge that you create your own miseries. God had to expel Adam and Eve from the garden. Unless you drop knowledge, I mean unless you are uncorrupted by knowledge, you cannot have the openness of a child. Where knowledge misses, innocence grasps. For a child, nothing is a problem to be solved. All is mystery. That is why a child keeps asking questions. A child is not afraid of mysteries. Only an adult is afraid. Acts of innocence and faith are acts of trust.

A child knows how to love. If you happen to cry in the presence of a child, the child won't argue with you and try to convince you that you are supposed to be happy. He just comes over and touches you. Nobody has a healing touch like a child's. Later in life, people become cold to others' pains, hardened, sophisticated, distant, calculating. But not children. A child's touch floods you with tenderness and softness, for his whole being is given to you in this innocent touch.

A child enjoys the world. A child knows how to play and have fun. A child knows that playing is a form of self-nourishment. Playing is serious business for a child. It transforms the boring day into the joyful day, the mundane into the sacred, the superficial into the essential.

A child does not worry about others' opinions. Maybe that is why all children are beautiful. Have you ever heard of an ugly child? An older person may become filled with memories and prejudices and disappointments and frustrations. A child has none of these. She is what she is and does not care about anything else. She lives here and now. She is at ease where she is and at rest with what she is. That is why her eyes have no anxieties. She knows little about duties, values, virtues, sins, sainthood. She exists before division and dualism and diversion and conflicts. She has no idea of good and bad. She lives life totally, wholly, passionately, unpredictably. Her desires are pure. A child is alive, full of promises, and enjoys grace and energy. She is beautiful. She lives in unity. She does not know how to be a hypocrite. She is genuine. She is what she is.

A child is closer to God than we are. He just came from God's home. He is still carrying God's fragrance. He is still authentic, simple, innocent, spontaneous, total, passionate, loving. Learn from his wonder and awe. Learn from his cheerfulness, joy, and life. As for the Kingdom of God, he is the master, not you. Look at life's reality through the eyes of a child. The moment you count on your own knowledge, you become a prisoner. A child has real eyes. He looks without obstruction, interpretation, experience, knowledge, or expertise. A child looks at the universe with eyes of wonder. The universe is wonderful to eyes that are wonderfilled. The eyes of a child create a new song in you. His eyes are full of intelligence and love. Somehow, a child is more intelligent when he starts his school years than when he graduates from college, when he has gone from love to knowledge. A child is straightforward, direct, in intimate relationship with the truth. Jesus stated it clearly: "Father, Lord of heaven and earth, to you I offer praise; for what you have hidden from the learned and the clever you have revealed to the merest children" (Matthew 11:25). Learn from a child. A child is close to God.

So, become like the child you once were. It is a requirement for entering the Kingdom of God.

ॐ

14

Poor in Spirit

If you accumulate too much knowledge, you may lose what is essential.

Nicodemus, the scholar, the man of virtues, the expert in interpreting the law, couldn't understand how one can be born of the Spirit (John 3:5-9). His knowledge prevented him from grasping this truth. He had a "rich" mind. Jesus did not say, "I am showing you the way and I am pointing out the truth to you and I am giving you life." He said, "I am the way, and the truth, and the life" (John 14:6). Mind alone does not fit with Jesus. Only one who has known death can follow Jesus. You must put at risk all of your past, all that you know, all that you have. You must empty yourself of greed, hate, violence, money, fame, and what-soever you can possess. At that moment, when you are poor in spirit, you become the most affluent, because the "Kingdom of heaven" is yours. The poorest becomes the richest. He has what is worth having.

If Jesus came today, I don't think He would recognize what theologians and philosophers are talking about, for He is so simple, so direct, so immediate. Those scholars are creating great sophisticated speculations, and have been doing so for two thousand years. They have created churches with all kinds of beliefs and different schools of thought. Jesus becomes lost. When one becomes uneasy – because one cannot comprehend Jesus – one creates theories about Him.

It is easier to deal with theories than with Jesus. Theories do not affect you much. You accumulate them in your mind. No danger. Jesus deals with your inmost secrets. He transforms you. You cannot stay the same. That is why unconsciously you feel safer and contented with what you can understand about Jesus. You think you can understand Him. You can build philosophies, including philosophies about Jesus, and you may be proud of them. But Jesus remains an outsider to your philosophies.

In a sense, most of what theology and philosophy say is false. Your theories are your inventions, and they become a wall between you and Him. They become more important than Jesus. That is why there are so many denominations in Christianity, so many faiths, so many conflicts, and so many "holy" wars. Jesus became secondary. Your theory about Jesus replaced Him.

To understand Jesus, you cannot be a "Christian," that is, you cannot have certain ideas about Him. Jesus will not fit into any of our theories or any of our plans. Jesus' presence breaks all limitations. To understand Jesus, you have to be "nobody." Only when you are "nobody" can you drop all the curtains that prevent you from seeing clearly. When your mind is empty, clear, clean, fresh, young, you will approach Jesus. Then there will be a divine meeting, and you will be transformed. Then you will start to know Him, as a friend, the Essential Friend.

Who came to listen to Jesus? Not to test Him, but to listen to Him? Think about it. Not a single rabbi did that. A rabbi has solutions and knows everything. Poor people – the uneducated, the uncultured – rushed toward Jesus: farmers, fishermen, gardeners, carpenters, the sick, the disabled. No one among his disciples was from a high class in society. No one was a priest. No one was a politician. No one was a professor, except Nicodemus. He was the last to understand Jesus, precisely because he was a professor. Judas was the most clever among the apostles, in charge of the finances. He chose to have the money instead of Jesus. Why did the learned people not come to Jesus? Not because Jerusalem was lacking in learned people. No. Jerusalem was at that time the seat of the Jewish university; people would come from far away to be educated in the city. Jerusalem was at a very high level. Those learned people believed they knew it all. They had read the Scriptures. They could quote wise sayings of the past. They possessed the right interpretations. Their memories were full. It is easy to imagine that their inflated egos were very far from accepting the idea of going to a carpenter's son who had nothing. He had no money, no fame, no certificate, no diploma – nothing. They were "rich." They didn't need to come to Jesus.

God is better known through subtraction than through addition and accumulation. You will have to drop many things before you can know God. You will have to be poor in spirit, like Abraham who left his belongings, his country, his heritage, his culture, his ways, his past, without knowing where he was heading (Hebrews 11:8). He made himself available to God, vulnerable, so open that he was ready to accept anything. "How blest are the poor in spirit" (Matthew 5:3), those who are ready to let themselves be penetrated by the word of God and ready to let their views, convictions, beliefs, systems, and lifestyles be reexamined and eventually changed. For Christ to be, "you" have to disappear.

Only the poor can escape from their egos and start something else because they know they cannot manage alone; they count on *someone* else, Jesus, their Essential Friend.

℘

15

Leave Your Father and Your Mother

Jesus asks His followers to leave everything, even their own fathers and mothers, symbols of their own inheritance, culture, and traditions. Not only that, He defined one aspect of His mission in these terms: "I have come to set a man at odds against his father, a daughter against her mother, a daughter-in-law against her mother-in-law; in short to make man's enemies those of his own household" (Matthew 10:35-36). "Do not suppose that my mission on earth is to spread peace. My mission is to spread, not peace, but division" (Matthew 10:34). Trenchant words, indeed, especially coming from somebody like Jesus, the "Prince of Peace." What is the essence of this message?

Jesus seems to be speaking contrary to traditions, all kinds of nationalism and fanaticism, and probably all kinds of "isms" and "ologies." Jesus' intention was to set Israel free from bondage to laws by opening ways to the new life of the Spirit. He wanted a new people of God, people who would be the nucleus of a new spiritual humanity. He did not reject the laws of Moses or the worship practices in the temple, but He broke down the barriers of exclusiveness and opened the door to new ways of being. He destroyed the wall in the temple that separated the Jews from the Gentiles, the holy people of God from the atheist people outside. And He broke down all walls of separation. "It is he who is our peace, and who made the two of us one by breaking down the barrier of hostility that kept us apart. In his own flesh he abolished the law with its commands and precepts, to create in himself one new man from us who had been two and to make peace, reconciling both of us to God in one body through his cross, which put that enmity to death" (Ephesians 2:14-16).

People opposed Jesus because He was destroying their edifices. He was uprooting all that they had protected for centuries. He rejected the traditions they loved and the values they cherished. His simple presence showed them that their houses were built on sand, not rock. The few individuals who remained with Him worried. His family, for example, asked Him to come back home. They wanted to bring Him to His senses. They wanted Him back in the system from which He liberated Himself and then distanced Himself. His inward journey to God the Father was so strong that He could ask His disciples later on to leave persons and things behind for the sake of His Kingdom. The old ways, the temple, this so-called religion, were going to fade away. He said, "Do you see all these buildings? I assure you, not one stone will be left on another – it will all be torn down" (Matthew 24:2). Jesus was not afraid to say whatever He wanted to say. Jesus took risks all the time, not only in His speech, but even in His lifestyle. He had no place to lay His head. He left His home to go on the road with new people. He visited sinners and trouble-makers. He left the security of invulnerability to join the human journey, risking failure. He lived in "tents," a symbol of shifting "truths," roles, relationships, ways of living, and meanings. He rejected harmony with the status quo. He wanted a conversion of the heart, a spiritual revolution, a faith that can move mountains. He knew that human beings do not change under pressure and external coercion. The new human being can come only from joy within. Jesus goes straight to the very core of life, intimately and whole-heartedly, the private then reflecting on the political and the public. He went to Jerusalem seeking to bring all humanity together, and there He was killed by the righteous elites. No other alternative. He was "too much" to be tolerated. His mission was to change the world by creating new hearts.

Should we imitate Jesus? Jesus asked His disciples to follow Him, not mimic Him. He asked them to learn from Him, to walk after Him, to follow Him on His inner journey to their inner selves where they can discover the Holy Spirit dwelling within, becoming true children of God, full of potential. To imitate Jesus is to live from within, as He did, to become other Christs, as He was, the same type of person, though with a different personality, a different history, in a different time. The real question for them and for us is not, Who *was* Jesus? but, Who *is* Jesus? The answer to the first question is relatively easy. You go into the library and you will find thousands of books about Jesus, and you will learn about Him and who He was historically. But you will not find the answer to the second question in the library. It can only be answered personally by each of us. Jesus is our Essential Friend on our faith journey. He shows the way. He is the Way.

How do you answer it yourself? How do I answer it myself? What does Jesus mean to me, here and now? Who *is* Jesus? Do we understand that He wants us to enter into the process that is going on in the world and give birth to a new, spiritual humanity? This would mean being open to others and having a genuine interest in their culture and heritage, in their social systems and their economic and global welfare, and helping them to overcome any oppression and any exploitation. To imitate Jesus means to make changes in the way we worship, carry on business, deal with people, and engage in politics. We should be able to revise all our systems and make them adequate to more justice and more love through a real partnership. This journey outward can only succeed when it proceeds inward first. We always need to turn inward to be with ourselves, in solitude, in the "deepest depths" of ourselves with the unspeakable presence of God. In this very center dwells God's own love. From there, we start to draw the picture of the new human being and the ultimate unification in world society, children of God living in peace.

Jesus was not only a prophet and a great teacher who left behind Him an ethical system of life. He is the Son of God, the second Adam, the principle of our strength and our own restoration to the divine likeness. He not only teaches us how Christian life is supposed to be, He creates it in us by the action of the Holy Spirit. And our life is no longer a mere moral perfection. It becomes an entirely new spiritual reality, a complete inner transformation. Just think of a human history without Jesus. There would have been no real fire in the world. Only Jesus can say, "Not one stone will be left on another" (Matthew 24:2). Only Jesus could come to destroy all temples because He knew that the true temple would be the human being himself. Only Jesus can push prayer and worship into second place, giving priority to justice and service to others. Only Jesus can exhort to go against the law and tradition and any kind of inheritance because His only law is to love one another. Only Jesus can say that we will not be judged for the number of religious practices we have made in our lifetime, but on the quality of our human relations. And only Jesus can make a drastic and uncompromising appeal such as this: "Whoever loves father or mother, son or daughter, more than me is not worthy of me" (Matthew 10:37).

How radical! How tough!

But look at it this way: "Know that I am with you always, until the end of the world" (Matthew 28:20), "for apart from me you can do nothing" (John 15:5).

80

16

The Art of Letting Go

Jesus was a model of letting go. He resisted any position He could have had in His society. He took advantage of no privilege, and He mixed with those who were considered to be lowest persons in society. He identified Himself with them. He frequented the desert, the sea, the mountain, and He relished solitude. He didn't hold to the image of what the Messiah ought to be, or of the kind of kingship he was supposed to have. He turned upside down the norms and values of His culture, especially the religious aspects of it. He didn't use miracles as a victory over or an intervention against nature in order to consolidate His power over others. The real miracle was not the trick of changing five loaves and two fishes into thousands. The real miracle consisted in teaching people to let go, to cease to be possessive, and to share. There is enough of everything to go around. When shared, things tend to multiply. The real miracle wasn't at kind of quantitative magical thing. It was kind of sharing and then letting go.

Jesus also preached the forgiveness of sins and the letting go of guilt. He preached forgiving our enemies and letting go of anger and greed. He entreated us to travel light on our life's journey, to be free of excess goods that leave no room for God.

Jesus Himself underwent a letting go, even of divinity, in order to be human. God did not intervene to save His divine Son from being crucified. Jesus underwent a divine void. He emptied Himself in order to become vulnerable to beauty and truth, to justice and compassion, to peace and love He allowed God, through Him, to burst into human history and human lives.

Jesus said, "Provide yourself with neither gold nor silver nor copper in your belts; no traveling bag, no change of shirt, no sandals, no walking staff" (Matthew 10:9-10).

The first thing to do is to let go of anxieties. Do not be anxious about superfluous things. To be anxious about them is a useless waste of time. Look at the flowers of the field and the birds of the sky. They are not anxious. They are taken care of. Do not look with anxiety into the future or into the past. They do not exist. Let them go. Live in the present. Do not be anxious about your thoughts, feelings, characters, images, concepts, or even knowledge. Do not cling to these furnitures of the mind. Let them go. Cling instead to the emptiness, the void, the "cloud of unknowing." Make room for God. Room means space, emptiness, thirst for the divine. When the furniture is removed, the room becomes filled with God's presence. Let go of your knowledge of God in order to let Him come dwell in you and reveal Himself to you as He is, not as you think He is. Surrender your attachment to thinking and enter into the silence of faith. God comes when you give in and become completely empty, when you can say, "I am no more," the "I" being all you gathered from others about yourself. Free yourself from the prison of others' opinions and from all your worldly possessions. The space occupied by those things belongs instead to the divine. Things are only substitutes. The more you feel possessive of things the less you can love. Love and space usually go hand in hand. It is rare to see love and riches combined together in one person, riches being material possessions as well as intellectual or spiritual possessions. Make room for God. God cannot be there if "you" still are, "you" being the sum of all the possessions you may have. These possessions stand in the way of God's entrance. Let them go. Only when you move away from yourself do you come to your true self. Only a total letting go of worldly possessions allows the divine to come forward and provide a glimpse of what is real.

You have little to lose by losing yourself. In fact, by doing this you gain yourself. Haven't you watched egotistical people? They can never let go of anything. They are poor people who happen to be in a state of possessing things. They are afraid of losing. They think all the time. When you are too obsessed by thinking, you cannot love because love is not a logical theory. Love is primarily a letting go of your attachments, your expectations, your preconceptions. When you look at things, always do it youthfully and with fresh eyes, as if for the first time. Let go of prejudices of all kinds. Do not interfere. When you are truly empty, all that you do will spring from the deepest source of existence.

The art of letting go is also the art of letting God happen.

℘

17

The Embrace

An embrace! Think of being embraced in love's name. Then think of being embraced in betrayal, "The man I shall embrace is the one; take hold of him" (Matthew 26:48). And Jesus was arrested.

Judas chose an embrace to identify the Master. An embrace, a sign of love, trust, and joy of life, became a betrayal, a poison, and a death sentence. Why did Judas choose to betray Jesus within an embrace?

An embrace!

Judas loved Jesus, not totally, but he loved Him. Judas had good times with Jesus. He had a very good position – in charge of the money, a position many would have loved to occupy. He was educated, cultured, skilled, polished, and belonged to a sophisticated society. He was not like the other disciples who were fishermen, farmers, carpenters, uneducated people, ordinary people, people of the earth. Judas was the most articulate in logic and thinking. He would like to be considered above others, to be recognized in the crowd. He wanted to be special. He was special. This is the trouble. Someone who feels special, superior to everyone else, usually allows him- or herself to do whatever is not allowed for others. John, his colleague, says that

"Judas held the purse, and used to help himself to what was deposed there" (John 12:6). When one is special, he can do that. His lie is not a lie; it is just a joke. His hypocrisy is not hypocrisy; it is a loyalty to what is right. His secret greed for power and money is not a greed for power and money; it is a search for the common good. So it goes. Judas tried many times to guide his Master. He had better arguments than the Master. When Mary at Bethany, for example, brought a jar of costly perfume and used it to anoint Jesus' feet, a strong protest came from Judas: "Why was not this perfume sold? It could have brought three hundred silver pieces, and the money have been given to the poor" (John 12:5). "What is the point of such extravagance? This could have been sold for a good price and the money given to the poor" (Matthew 26:8-9; see also Luke 7:37-38).

Who can argue with the necessity of helping the poor? Isn't this a very solid argument? Doesn't this sound familiar? A capitalist can use this argument. A socialist can use it. An independent can use it too. But Jesus has another view. He was not interested in the money, neither was He interested in perfumed oil. He was interested in the heart of that woman and her conversion. She was coming with a prayer, a song, and much love in her heart. And this is what really matters. The head would not understand this. The head has its own reasons, different from the reasons of the heart. The heart's reasons are very subtle. One needs special eyes to see. Judas knew nothing about the heart. He was blind to the woman and her heart. He looked only at the perfume and saw how costly it was. This is what a thinker does. He calculates. Judas was a thinker, an economist, a philosopher. He was convinced of the fact that he had a deeper understanding than Jesus.

Judas was certainly hurt. His ego was hurt. He gave the right advice to Jesus, and Jesus didn't listen to him.

He wanted the common good of the poor, and through this artificially good gesture, he wanted to satisfy his greed for power – his advice would have worked – and for money – he would have gotten his hands on more money. At the Last Supper, he must have been very happy to have the Master washing his feet. He was waiting for such a gesture, such a unique and "humbling" occasion for the Master.

Judas loved money. But money was not really the only or most important reason for the conspiracy. He was too intellectual and too refined to be satisfied with just thirty pieces of silver. He must have had a more profound reason: when Jesus was gone, he would be in charge. Deep down, he was expecting to overthrow Jesus and take over His position. He wanted to be the head of the whole community. After all, wasn't he more educated and more cunning than Jesus? He needed to remove Jesus from the scene. He could not assassinate Him, but he could sell Him. Then he would have both the money and the power he really wanted. Why not? He was, after all, a "good" man. He was the most qualified, and he knew how to follow the logic of the mind and the code and rules of the society's games. He was a politician, which Jesus was not. What can you expect from someone who says something like, "Love your enemies, pray for your persecutors" (Matthew 5:44). "Do to others what you would have them do to you" (Luke 6:31). "Be on guard against performing religious acts for people to see" (Matthew 6:1). "Do not lay up for yourselves earthly treasure" (Matthew 6:19). "Nothing is concealed that will not be revealed, and nothing hidden that will not become known" (Matthew 10:26). "What profit would a man show if he were to gain the whole world and destroy himself in the process?" (Matthew 16:26). "Whoever wants to rank first among you must serve the needs of all" (Matthew 20:27). "You shall love your neighbor as yourself" (Matthew 22:29). "Say, 'Yes' when you mean 'Yes' and 'No' when you mean 'No" (Matthew 5:37), and so forth. This is not politics in this world of ours. Jesus was, for the world we have created, the worse "politician" ever to exist. Judas could be a successful leader and a good master in this world of ours. Jesus, the Master, is an unqualified leader and a poor master. He was a patent failure in this world of ours. He managed to end up dying on the cross.

Judas represents the ego. Judas knows to compute, make compromises, lobby (Matthew and Luke did not name Judas at the event of Bethany, saying only, "when the disciples saw this they grew indignant, protesting"), and win. Jesus, here, is a loser. Judas can be a crafty business-person, a foxy lawyer, a cunning and phony religious minister, or just an ordinary, greedy, opportunistic liar. Jesus can only be simple, direct, straightforward, and 'naive' – innocent. Judas exists in each of us. We are disciples of Jesus, as Judas was. We love Jesus, as Judas loved Him. And we hate Jesus, at the same time, as Judas hated Him. When you love someone, a part of you is going to be somewhat hurt because love requires a total surrender. When you move toward a total surrendering, somehow a certain uneasiness arises. The ego resists. The ego starts to calculate. The power, the money, the prestige – the false self – are at stake. That part in us that becomes troubled by unconditional love is Judas. You start to think that "it is costly," "we could have used this for the common good." A Judas will give you the best speech on love. He will create a perfect how-to book on love. But he does not love because love is total trust. Trust is too risky for him. Judas loved Jesus, but not totally. He was very divided. He lived a tragic dichotomy. To be able to betray, you must love first. No wonder he used the embrace as a signal. An embrace, a loving gesture, became a gesture of hate. The embrace translates very well the terrible dichotomy he was in, the split, the divided personality. As soon as Jesus was arrested and condemned, Judas committed suicide. Jesus, the object of his love and hate, was gone. And so was the meaning of his life. Emptiness leads to suicide, or, at least, to a continuous unhappiness. This is what happens to some of those who are most articulate in logic and in thinking. The most learned people and the richest people, if they do not have love in their hearts, are also the most miserable people. Intellect, as important as it is, never satisfies a human being. The heart does. The mind can betray. Real love cannot betray. The mind agrees with Judas, the heart agrees with Jesus. The followers of Judas are in the millions, because it does not cost much. Judas would say, "If you follow me, I'll give you this or that." The real followers of Jesus are just a few because they have to pay – with their lives, their very being. It is too risky! But when you pay it all, you have it all too.

Wherever a Jesus is, a Judas will be there too. "The way, and the truth, and the life" (John 14:6) are so tremendous, so demanding that someone, in fact many, are bound to betray. The ego won't yield easily. The ego won't let the good heart succeed and obtain control. If the good heart succeeds, the ego will be destroyed. So, it is better, from the ego's point of view, to get rid of the goodness of the heart, at any price, even for thirty pieces of silver, and let goodness be on the cross.

Judas loved Jesus and hated Him too. He embraced Him. That ambiguous embrace was the beginning of Christ's crucifixion.

Are you a divided person, a person of compromises? Do you have a split personality? Does unconditional, total love mean anything to you? Is the love in your life real? What kind of embrace do you offer to your family, to your friend, to your neighbor, to a stranger – Jesus?

What does your embrace really mean in your heart?

ॐ

18

Change

Do you intend to change the world? First, you must change your perception and your belief system.

Life is much broader than a single theory. Life is so vast that it contains all theories, contradictions, possibilities, opportunities, and dreams.

To live is to change.

The idea – the pure idea (in Plato's sense) – can possibly remain unchangeable. But when you come to live the idea, there is no way to keep it safe from changing and becoming.

Doing is becoming, isn't it?

We do. We become. We learn. We change. We grow.

Change is the only permanent thing in life. Seasons change. Mornings come. Evenings come. Days change into nights. Nights change into days. Childhood changes. Our moods, ideas, feelings change, even if we rarely pay attention to this kind of change because we are too much involved in it. Life is simply a phenomenon of change. Do you remember Heraclitus for whom life is a flux, a river. Can you step into the same river twice? The same river is never the same twice.

Change keeps increasing, every day, with continuously accelerating speed. Even the news you've just read becomes old history in a matter of hours.

Everything, after all, can be challenged. Any doctrine, any discipline, any law, any custom, even "God" Himself as we understand Him can be challenged. Are we sure that when we talk about God we talk really about the same God, not about our own interpretation of God or what we have been taught about Him?

The church also has its historical development, and therefore it has been subject to continual change. The Jewish-Greek-Roman basis is not the only possible way that the Spirit uses to work. The Spirit has thousands of different ways. Let Him work. Don't interfere. Let grace give life to the law, and let the spirit vitalize the letter.

The organization, of course, is necessary. But to remain meaningful, and in order to serve its original purpose, this organization has continually to renew itself, to find new ways of expressing its doctrines. Keeping itself rigid and stereotyped won't fit with the creative fires of the Holy Spirit. Structures can be only if they become. They exist when they are allowed to change. Change is an inherent quality of a structured life.

When you really believe, you don't only interpret history. You change it. Grace uses human freedom to change history. God is always new, always fresh, always unexpected. This is how He was in the past. This is how He is now. This is how He will be in the future. We have only a partial knowledge of His plan and purpose, and also a partial knowledge of the universe. It is needless, then, to say that every ontology, as well as everything based on this ontology, will always remain temporary and open to continuous revision. Thus, every norm is open to revision as the Spirit moves our freedom in history and makes us see things with new approaches of His wisdom and surprising aspects of

His power. It is even atheistic to pretend that, at a certain age or time, a person or a structure cannot change anymore, as it is an unforgivable sin to believe that the "old self" of Paul cannot be renewed and transformed on a new one (2 Corinthians 4:16; Ephesians 4:23; Colossians 3:10).

We cannot understand God if we are rigid. As situations change, our understandings must change too, otherwise we lose our understanding. By staying the same, we betray the very reality that we wanted to keep the same. Every few years, we have to retranslate a book, even and maybe especially the Bible. Every few years, we have to rewrite a dictionary. The same words don't convey the same message in succeeding situations and for different generations.

There is nothing on earth that is perfect. Nothing is supposed to be perfect. No human being is perfect either. Perfection, except in God, means death. The moment you quit your journey, you die. If being perfect means that you stop growing and changing, because there is nothing left to be done, nowhere left to go, and no other possibility to explore, you are dead. Keep moving, don't strive for perfection, never stop trying. Then God is alive in you.

The continuous call to repent is a summons and a convocation to a complete and radical change of life, both for the individual and for the society. It is an invitation to a permanent newness of life. The Christian order is such a dynamic order that only the Spirit knows what the next step will be. Allow God to work and the energy of life to flow. Let your hands become God's hands. Let your feet become God's feet. Let your eyes become God's eyes. You will see things in totally different ways. Everything has changed, not because things are not the same anymore, but because *you* have changed, you have been transformed.

So, the fact of changing activities is not going to change your world, the world. A new activity does not mean necessarily a new life. The real change is in *you*. People go on changing jobs, hobbies, wives, husbands, cars, religions, and whatever can be changed, with the hope that this time something is going to happen, that happiness is at hand. The reality is that nothing is going to happen unless *you* change. Only inner change can transform something. Give up the ambition to change things. When you change your consciousness, things will change by themselves. By transforming yourself, you transform the world. When you are reborn, the world is reborn too. The same things are not the same things anymore. They now have a different color, your color.

As you change your perception, the whole world will change accordingly.

God has created the world and continues to create it through us – our minds, hearts, ordinary lives, and everyday activities. He speaks through artists, poets, theologians, psychologists, developers, businesspersons, legislators, a flower, a song, a prayer, any technological wonder. He made us cocreators. With Him, we make things happen. The Holy Spirit, within and with us, changes us, and changes things around us, and changes the world.

෨

19

Rejoice!

What has happened to joy? What has happened to fun? What has happened to games played just for the pleasure of playing rather than the drive to win? What has happened to belly laughter shared with a friend? And why must we always say, "When this or that happens, then I will be happy?" Why must the fullness of life be always around the corner, in the promotion we are expecting, or that trip we intend to make, or that relationship we are looking for?

Everyone has the right and the need to be happy. Everyone is entitled to this happiness. But the person who seeks happiness as a goal will usually not find it because happiness is not a thing that we possess. Whenever a person, a society, a civilization seeks happiness elsewhere, it will not be found. Joy is not like a drug. People take things forget themselves. People do not want to face their problems and their miseries. A drug helps them forget that misery, temporarily. The same thing can be said about one who counts too much the "good old days" or the "wonderful tomorrows," that house I'll build, that trip I'll make, that job I really want, that relationship so much expected, or that God to please by just performing external "religious" acts. All these things, like drugs, provide perhaps a little consolation by helping us to forget and to escape ourselves. Joy is not found in external circumstances and things. Joy is found within us.

Unless you are happy within yourself, in your unique true self and in your ordinariness, right now, right here in the particular circumstances you are in, no matter what, you will never be happy. Happiness is in you. You are happy when you know yourself as you are and not because of something that has happened to you. You are happy just to be, to breathe, to walk, to eat, to sleep, and to wake up for a new day. If you are not happy in these little ordinary things, you will take your dissatisfaction with you to the "heaven" you dream of. Wherever you are and whatever goals you achieve, they do not make big differences. You will carry your world of sadness and darkness with you because this world you carry is within you, not outside of you.

Real happiness is not something superficial. True happiness is a deep joy, the pure joy of being. There are times when we feel closer to the universe and to God, we feel part of the whole. These times are to be treasured. They are unitive. They are "timeless." They transcend limitations, frontiers, and dichotomies. The times of deep joy are independent of outside events. We do not have this kind of joy because something has happened. We have this joy because life is joyful. We feel alive. We enjoy God by personal encounter. In God's presence we learn to be still, to listen, and to contemplate. There we have no practical goal to achieve, and we do not strive to get anywhere. Just being in the here and now and feeling alive to God and His world. When Martha, in the gospel, was very busy preparing dinner, Mary, her sister, was sitting still – listening, looking, experiencing, loving, and doing nothing. Wherever we are, we should learn to be still, to learn by entering into the mystery of things, the mystery of a pink-colored sunset, a dark green hill, a peaceful lake, a shaky blade of grass, an inspiring poem, a beautiful symphony, a playful dog, or the impressive flight of a bluebird. The hidden God is in each and every one of these little things. Inner joy brings not only a personal satisfaction, but it helps to change our perception of ourselves and of our relationships to our world and to God. Inner joy is a real inner shift. It enhances our ability to love and our enthusiasm for living, and it allows us to make greater contributions. Real love happens when we are full of joy. So being still does not mean necessarily a retreat from living life fully and intensely. It means, rather, that we should bring to everything a joyful dimension of depth and of appreciation. It means that we should do whatever we are doing with all our might and heart. Like Jesus, we should be engaged totally with the special reality of the persons we meet and the situations we encounter. Do we really feel the neighbor's pain? Do we really share that family's joy? Do we really walk an extra mile to help settle a conflict? Do we say a word of consolation and encouragement to Carol who just lost her job? Do we really help Bob to find a better job so that he is better able to support his five children, wife, and mother? Deep joy is more in giving than in getting something. Deep joy is not evasive. It is very precise. It knows *every* nuance of the human heart and mind, and it cares about all the details of any situation. Deep joy is right here, right now – never there and never in the past nor in the future. The "there," the past and the future, are not real. We read the "there," the past and the future, through the prism of our present. If we are depressed now, we see unpleasant things in the past and in the future. If we are full of joy now, we will see our good memories and our future growth. Thus we have all advantages to fill the present with joy and let other times and places be. "Do not worry" (Matthew 6:25). They most likely are abstractions. The more contemplative, the more active.

Joy, therefore, is a powerful drive. It means saying yes! to life when we have reason to say no. This positive willingness is in no way an uncritical affirmation of distorted earthly conditions. No! The positive willingness is also a willingness to act and make the lives of others acceptable. Christian joy means love, and it means nothing without love. Christian joy is a fullness of life. Jesus said, "I came that they might have life and have it to the full" (John 10:10). Saint Irenaeus would echo this by saying, "The glory of God is a human being who is fully alive!" So life should not be a battlefield, where competition, jealousy, and greed are the masters that take away our blooming. Life should be joy and celebration. Let's grow more flowers. Let's spread more love and laughter. A hand that plants a rose cannot drop a bomb on a city. A loving hand cannot keep a gun loaded with anger, hatred, and death. Joyful hearts prevent wars. They reach the Ultimate in an easier and more direct way. They are more contemplative. They are more active.

Joy is the most adequate sign of the presence of God. "Rejoice in the Lord always! I say it again. Rejoice!" (Philippians 4:4). Christianity is a "joyful message." It is a good news of a great rejoicing (Luke 2:10-14).

Rejoice and pray with these or similar words: "O God, my Father, don't let me die without having really lived and having really loved!"

ℰꝎ

20

The Sacrifice of Being Happy

The greatest sacrifice is probably the sacrifice of being happy. Joy is much more difficult to live than sadness.

The secret of being happy is to be grateful – grateful to God for what He did for us. Isn't gratitude the very meaning of our religion? Religion is not really the number of things we do for God, but the recognition of what He did and continues to do for us.

I don't know why we hold on to this tendency to see Christ on the cross. To see Christ only crucified does not suggest that we've accepted the transition from death to life, from sin to grace, from old to young, from tradition to spontaneity, from stagnation to creativity, from the old order to the new order, from the "many things" to the "one necessary thing," from the old self to the new self, our transformation.

Somehow, in our deepest soul's core, we would like to look sad. We have a tendency toward pessimism, for always seeing the dark side of things, for being pleased in anxieties and worries, for reading about catastrophes, and even for seeing others in difficulties, as if we possess an unconscious bitterness and a certain kind of inner rancor.

It seems easier to grieve with a friend than to associate with him or her in joy.

In joy, there is a subtle detachment. We detach first from our ego. To share a joy with another is not to recognize that person's greater value and thus defer to him or her, sometimes to our detriment. We can never be happy until we let go of our ego. This letting go is our ultimate sacrifice, but this sacrifice brings our greatest joy.

To be happy in spite of the odds is something painful and grievous. It requires us to accept our human condition, which we were trying to evade. To be happy means that we cannot receive joy if we do not produce it in others.

Gratitude! To be happy is to be grateful for who and what we are, as well as for those things that we have. Are we aware of what God did for us? Are we aware of the gifts of our senses, the capacity to move, our own freedom, our health, our family and friends, and all those little things that we take for granted until we miss them? Our gratitude to God is to give Him the joy of seeing us happy daily.

Gratitude! To be happy is to look at what God has made, the way He looked Himself when He created the world. "God looked at everything he had made, and he found it very good" (Genesis 1:31).

Gratitude! To be happy is to share God's joy and to tell Him that we cannot live without His love anymore.

ℰℴ

21

On Laughter

Laughter may be the right answer to the play of existence. Perhaps Chamfort was right when he said, "The most wasted day is that in which we have not laughed." H. L. Mencken got it right when he said, "One horse-laugh is worth ten thousands syllogisms. It is not only more effective; it is also vastly more intelligent."

Only through laughter can one understand life, never through seriousness. Seriousness is the disease of the ego. A serious person cannot celebrate life with dance and songs and joys. How far is the ego from life! Life is better understood through laughter.

Only a human being can laugh. Animals don't laugh. A computer does not laugh. Things do not laugh. Only persons laugh. And you can know a person from his laugh. Dostoevsky said it: "One can know a man from his laugh, and if you like a man's laugh before you know anything of him, you may confidently say that he is a good man."

Laughter is a peak in your own growth. It is a religious act. It is a prayer of gratitude. It is a bridge to reach the Ultimate Truth. Laughter is a celebration of life.

One may have a tendency to laugh about others. This is a part of the ego, a very superficial thing. A "serious" laughter makes sense when one starts to laugh at oneself in the first place, and at his system of beliefs.

Only mystics can have a real belly laugh. They are free.

How can you laugh if you are burdened with all kinds of theories, ideologies, theologies, philosophies, and all kinds of seriousness? How can you laugh if you cannot laugh at the ridiculousness of all these things?

One has theories about everything. He knows too much. She has hundreds of speculations about religion while missing the essential point: religion has to be *lived*.

The ridiculousness of things! What is the meaning of studying theories about food and how to prepare them if you so hungry? Do you live on theories? When theoreticians enter the field of truth, truth disappears. Theories take over. What a joke!

Why do you laugh when you hear a joke, anyway? Because the story in a joke takes a sudden turn. What happens is not what you were expecting. It is illogical. See? You expect truth and you have theory. A thoughtful, sensitive person cannot but laugh at all that.

Only laughter frees you and brings maturity to your life. On the physical level, laughter, according to science, is the best medicine nature has provided to human beings. If you are sick, laughter will bring back your health sooner. And if you are in good health, laughter maintains your health longer. Laughter aids digestion, stimulates the heart, strengthens muscles, and activates the brain's creativity. When you are joyful and happy, you feel more open to life and more capable of handling tension. Laughter is a natural painkiller because it causes the body to secrete a special hormone that prevents you from feeling pain. Laughter exercises your heart and protects it.

Laughter makes you feel unified. Divisions in you disappear. Body, mind, heart, and soul join hands again.

Laughter can be the path to wholeness and holiness. Solemnity is not a virtue. A good laugh is. A deep, satisfying laugh brings you closer to the divine. This is, essentially, what life is all about.

§

22

Communication

When we are foreigners to others, we are also foreigners to ourselves and to God.

When we look at things, inhale fresh air, eat, drink, work, we mean to say, in fact, that all the universe must be friendly, necessary, part of us.

Human beings live in the material world by exchanging things. Other kinds of communication are more important. Human beings are created to be in relation. We may even say that relationships make human beings.

Confidence, affection, and tenderness help us to accept ourselves and keep going. They are major factors for growth.

One does not reach out through ideas only, or by understanding. One reaches out through experiences lived by the whole personality. A real word, from the depths, is required.

When you pray, do you speculate? No! You use your heart to pray. The heart is the true means for communication with people and – especially – with God.

People do anything to establish communication. They construct roads and bridges. They invent cars and planes. They install telephones and televisions. They organize meetings and conferences. They send letters. They produce magazines. They write books. They try and try and try to abolish distances between one another. But distance, somehow, remains. It may even increase because the real gap is of another order.

Jesus had different ways of communicating with people. He went straight to their hearts. Prejudices based on race, family status, religion, class, or even social rules of morality were left behind. His primary concern was to awaken the true self in everyone, initiating a new start. How many were waiting for a word from Him? "Speak the word only, and my servant shall be healed" (Matthew 8:8). "The man put his trust in the word Jesus spoke to him, and started for home" (John 5:50).

Can you imagine what a power we have on others and what a power they have on us!

How many people are waiting for that appropriate word to restore a life and start living again!

A real word, emerging from your heart, speaks to another heart. It bridges the gap of the invisible distance. It unmasks lies and hypocrisies. It touches. It transforms. One is changed when one communicates the word of truth from the heart.

The quality of our communication with others is so important that it will be the basic criterion for our last evaluation (Matthew 25:31-46).

Our communication with others defines our communication with God and what we really are.

ॐ

23

Right Rather Than Righteous

Genuineness is a quality of a *right* person. Politics is part of a *righteous* lifestyle.

A right person moves according to his inner world. He is in tune with himself. He is unified. He does not need to be a crowd. He does not pretend. He is true to himself and to others. He says yes when he means it and no when he means it. His behavior translates what is going on within him. He is the worst politician imaginable.

A righteous person, when he is not right, is a very dangerous person. He is false, phony, and hypocritical. He lives a double life: one for the world and one for himself. He possesses the art of hiding things. He tells you what you want to hear. His truth does not spring from principle. His truth corresponds to an external statistic and keeps an eye on the popular vote. He is a politician. He handles situations very well. He lives before the eyes of others. His reference is in his appearance and in the mask he wears. He is the most sophisticated, egotistical person in the world. He is moralistic. Deep down, he is able to condemn everybody. His morality is based on fear of punishment and hell, and maybe on greed – his eye remains fixed on the rewards he can get from others and, later on, in heaven. His behavior, instead of being an outcome of what he is, is the source of his action. He follows the rules. He who wants to play has to follow certain rules. A moralistic person plays the game of society. He follows the rules of the game. People believe he is religious because he often goes to the church and gives money to the poor. He knows how to gain respectability. He succeeds in wrapping himself in religiosity, even if his religion is only politics. His religion is part of his struggle to survive, part of his ambition, and a means of controlling others.

A righteous person is led by the law, although law is not that bad after all. A right person is led by love.

Law is important to society and helps us to live in the world. But love is much more important to society and gives us, from outside the world, the reason to be in the world. Something from the invisible is needed. Law may come by logic, interest, and practicality. Love springs from mystery and the unknown and the human heart.

By following the law, you are safe, respected, and righteous. By acting with love, your life will be poetry and dance. Law is your house. Love is your home. If you are lawful and nothing else, you will not be able to love anybody because you lack spontaneity and magic.

You can prove the existence, necessity, and appropriateness of the law; it is usually a scientific matter. But how to prove love? Love is antiscience, antilogic and very often beyond law. A great scientist can love, can be full of love, but he can never prove it in his lab. Law makes you proud of yourself and your knowledge. Love makes you humble, and reveals to you that you still do not know much about the real truth.

If you live by the law, you are going to be successful in the world. That is for sure. And if you live by love, misfortune is your fate. In the world, law succeeds, not love. People who live by calculations find that nobody can compete with them. They are successful in business, in politics, even in religion. People who live by love are sometimes failures. Law is social, dependable, secure. Love is wild, insecure, dangerous, and mad. Law makes you a good citizen and dictates to you how to behave with others. Love makes you a good person and tells you how to behave yourself in the first place. Law can be the foundation of the society, but it can never be the spirit of it. Law is needed so that love becomes possible. The end is not the law, but love. Moses, who provided the law, was fulfilled by Jesus who provided us divine love, graces, and eternal truths. Law does not really prove God's existence. Only love does. God is love.

The norm of true morality is not, in the final analysis, fidelity to the law, but fidelity to the Spirit, that is, fidelity to the law of love that includes the other law, since "love is the fulfillment of the law" (Romans 13:10).

A right person reaches exactly this point. He is true to himself, to others, and to God, no matter what, even if he ends up on the cross, like Jesus. A righteous person prefers to be on the side of the secure law, no matter what, because he knows very well that this is the right way to be successful in the world, even if he is, often, the very cross.

Jesus was never more severe than with the righteous people, the Pharisees and Scribes. "The scribes and the Pharisees have succeeded Moses as teachers; therefore, do everything and observe everything they tell you. But do not follow their example. . . . Woe to you scribes and Pharisees, you frauds!"(Matthew 23).

Only genuine people are accepted in the Kingdom of God, no matter how sinful their lives may have been. A deep morality of love is required. For the Kingdom, to be righteous is not enough. One is required to be right, genuine, authentic, and loving others with the very love of Jesus.

こ

24

The Imperfection of Being a Perfectionist

Being a perfectionist is not what we should be in life. It is not the ideal to be sought. We are not picture straighteners on the wall. Our life is neither a stationary attitude, nor a static point of equilibrium where everything seems quiet and peaceful. Our life shows us eloquently that when we reach the top of something we don't stop, we keep going.

A perfectionist can be a joyless person who does not know how to laugh, play, have fun, or share love. His world is not real. He lives in his head, according to his mind.

A perfectionist is very often the hardest-working person around. There is nothing wrong with working hard, but the perfectionist's "efficiency" brings misery to himself and to others. Progress results not from trying to be perfect, but from trying to be better. A perfectionist wants to be perfect, but perfection is an illusion. It leads nowhere. Our human condition compels us to a lifelong need to ask questions, to ask for help. A perfectionist won't usually show ignorance. On the contrary, he has this tendency to show that he knows something before he's told. A perfectionist does not present himself as he really is. He likes to see himself as "perfect" in the eyes of others, and maybe in his own eyes as well. The truth is that a perfectionist is usually the least able to approach either perfection or excellence in his life and work. A perfectionist wastes too much energy making sure that his proficiency and performance are known. Then he is very careful not to embark on any activity that involves risk. Only an imperfect person does not expect success all the time. He can learn from his failures too. An imperfect person dares to ask preliminary questions and never expects final answers. A perfectionist pretends. There is a lot of pride, and even violence, in his attitude.

A perfectionist is always dissatisfied with life and with other people. He is always anxiously pursuing tomorrow and the next thing to do, to buy, to look at, to appear to be. But tomorrow and the next thing never come. A perfectionist is skilled in identifying reasons why conditions around him are not at the level he deserves.

A perfectionist cannot really love easily and cannot really be easily loved. Withdrawn into her ivory tower of fears, she does not give others the chance to understand her, nor does she understand them. She who sees only what others should be is not ready to see who they really are. And if she marries, that marriage will, without doubt, end in divorce, because she marries her image of the spouse, not the person himself as he is. The image does not last long. We cannot love unless we accept that person, unless we become real and realistic.

A perfectionist lives under the tyranny of "should." From birth to death, our life is surrounded by advice, warnings, all kinds of pulls and pushes from and toward what we should or should not do with tomorrow. From early childhood, a child is immersed in the "shoulds" of perfection. A perfectionist is one who never succeeds in liberating herself from this infantile attitude, unintentionally becoming a dictator toward herself and toward others.

A perfectionist hates to make enemies, for to make enemies is a failure. He is supposed to be nice, and nice people do not have enemies. What an illusion! The fact is that the "greatest" people are often the most hated of their generation, precisely because they take a stand. A perfectionist prefers to be on the safe side, to keep the peace. Only people who know how to "make enemies" leave an impact on human history. A perfectionist has no enemies, nor does he have any real friends either.

A perfectionist is jealous. She expects people to respond in a certain way. She has specific requirements. She thinks that jealousy is a "proof" of caring, a kind of thermometer by which to gauge the heat of love. Real love has nothing to do with jealousy. The more we love the less we feel jealous. Jealous people do not love others; they love only receiving what they think they deserve from others. So does the perfectionist.

We need to realize, in a very concrete way, that we should make a decision to take charge of our imperfect selves, in our imperfect world. You can never be perfect. You can always improve on whatever you do. And if you happen to think that what you have done is perfect, you have lost your imagination. You are finished with living. Imperfection keeps you going. Perfection should be a process, not a state of being. So improve, be better, become whole, but never fall into perfectionism. And know that God is in the real, rather than in the ideal. God, whose definition is "I am who am" (Exodus 3:14), is found in anything which is real even if that reality is the weakness of our human condition. The "I am who am" can never be encountered in some nonexistent expectations or far-flung ideals. "I am who am" is here right now.

Perfectionism is imperfect in a real spiritual life.

ॐ

25

On Growth

I am glad to be imperfect; I have the chance to grow. Only with my imperfections is growth possible! Life is a phenomenon of growth. Anything that grows is imperfect; otherwise, how will it grow?

But there is a price to pay: the risk in growing. Growing up is a transformation, a change, a progression from less maturity to more maturity. Growing up is not easy. Many people won't do it. Many adults, even successful adults, remain psychologically infantile until they die. Growth is an invitation to the unknown in life. And this is what makes us truly alive. A full life is going to be full of joy and full of pain. Otherwise, it is not a life really lived.

Growth is a sort of detachment. To refuse the real fact of growth, as some psychologists say, causes complexes, psychological retardations, and neuroses. It is a refusal to leave the mother's womb, the sad security of the Platonic cave. Growth is a detachment from these old patterns of infantilism. Shouldn't we link moral virtues to global growth rather than to the oceanic security of an unreal paradise! The notion of static virtues is disappearing with time. People, at the present state of consciousness, are starting to speak about virtue and vice in terms of growth rather than of solid concepts or of a certain urge of returning to a psychic life of childhood. A certain emotional maturity seems essential for a moral virtue. One must grow. One must accept the fact of detachment from old infantilisms. Many vices or "virtues" are simply a result of a lack of growth in a deeper level of our psyche. Virtue should lead us to a further union and a deeper communion. Growth is a detachment even from our "virtues." A human being has a duty to unglue himself from infantilism, to detach himself from patterns, and to continually grow and mature. One cannot rest. There is no static state in life. If you don't move forward, you are moving backward. The only rest there is comes through detachment and growth.

Growth is God's way of working in the world. The creation is not finished yet. The Creator has not chosen to create things at once. He rather has elected to remain intimately and mysteriously involved in all aspects of creation – especially our lives. "The Spirit . . . remains with you and will be within you" (John 14:17). There is no escape from the creative, sustaining Spirit (Psalm 139:7). He is the immanent force within every creature. He gives new hearts (Ezekiel 36:26). He is the principle of a new life. Those who receive Him walk according to Him (Galatians 6:8), are led by Him (Romans 8:4), are filled with His gifts and fruits (Galatians 5:22-23), and are helped by Him to open their hearts and minds to the mysteries of God (1 Corinthians 2:10-16). "The Paraclete, the Holy Spirit whom the Father will send in my name, will instruct you in everything, and remind you of all that I told you" (John 14:26). He will therefore show us the truth, not immediately evident, of future things and the definitive plan of salvation. He allows us to grow. He fills us with vitality. The Spirit is present in us as spiritual vitality and growth. This is why our striving to achieve holiness should not be understood as reaching a static "state of perfection." No! Holiness is an ongoing process that animates our daily lives, here and now. It is the experience of God who is at work in the world today. This means that we should be able, at the personal level as well as at the community level, to let go what we *were* and be ready to accept and *be* what the Spirit wants us to be. The Spirit dwells in the vitality of persons much more than in any specific structure. By opening our hearts and minds to the Spirit, we will prove that the Incarnation was not an isolated historical event in time and history, but a continuous phenomenon that goes on anytime, anywhere. The Spirit is the newness at work in the world. His presence affects deeply not only the consciousness and hearts of individuals, but also society, history, peoples, cultures, and especially religions. "The Spirit of God with marvelous foresight directs the course of the ages and renews the face of the earth" (*Gaudium et Spes,* 26). The Spirit is our growth. He is our wholeness and our holiness.

Growth, therefore and above all, is a spiritual phenomenon. Growing up is different from growing old. Growing old is physical. Your body grows old. But your being cannot grow old. Your being will grow up or it may choose to remain immature. Growing up extends into consciousness and into the core of your being. You grow deep within yourself. The deeper the roots in the ground, the stronger the tree will be and the higher it will go. Your roots should keep going deeper and deeper until they reach the ground of your being – God. God is your growth. You have no real fulfillment except the experience of God. You have no real growth outside God-love. Wherever you see love, aliveness, sprouts, growth, God is there. Only God "grows." In everything, God grows. Wherever you find growth, be careful. Come closer. Be cautious. Feel fully and deeply. Open your eyes and ears and mind and heart and soul. You are on a holy ground.

ॐ

26

What Makes a Saint?

Can one be a saint in the marketplace? Is the one who renounces the world a saint? Is the one who denies the pleasures of life and practices all kinds of asceticisms automatically a saint? Is the hermit who prays all day long a saint? Is the one who spends his entire life in a monastery destined to be a saint? Is the one who rises high in the hierarchy, serving the church well with the greatest zeal, a saint? What are the characteristics of true sanctity?

The first thing that pops into our mind is that sanctity must be associated with asceticism. We have a tendency to think that the more one gives up, the closer one is to God, and therefore to sanctity. Attaining sanctity demands the renunciation of food, comfort, pleasures, expensive clothes, shelter, and anything that feels comfortable – simply saying "no" to life. The ascetic renounces it, denounces it, condemns it, tries to hate it.

But does not asceticism appeal more strongly to the ego than to sanctity as such? The ego is greatly reinforced by the number of "no's" with which it can surround itself. A saint should renounce this very ego rather than denounce the world.

A saint should not become an island – independent, separate from the world; he is part of the whole. Reality is the saints' participation, not isolation, a "yes" to life, not a "no" to all that is.

God's work is beautiful and joyous. Look at it! Look at these trees, these flowers, these birds, this sky, these stars. Aren't they just divine, filled with the holy? Enjoy them! Celebrate life! Be grateful to the Lord, who will ask you one day, What did you do with the many gifts I have given you? Why haven't you shared them with others? I have given you the gift of loving; what have you done with it? What you must renounce is not the world, but your selfish ego. "I do not ask you to take them out of the world, but to guard them from the evil one" (John 17:15).

The ego is the way of the world. The ego is reinforced by riches, power, possessions. The ego can go with you wherever you go, even to the monastery or the hermitage, regardless of your situation in life, even if you become a preacher or a bishop. You may renounce the world, but your ego is there. With the selfish ego, sanctity is just an illusion. The real way to renounce the ego is to celebrate. In bliss, in joy, in ecstasy your ego disappears. When you laugh, you forget yourself. In sadness your ego comes back to you. Dance! In a real dance, the dancer disappears; only the dance remains. The world has to be rejoiced over and loved deeply. Isn't that what God has made? God "saw how good it was" (Genesis 1:25, 31). So delight in it. Through delight you will gain glimpses of the creator in the creation. A true saint is always happy – happy to be in God's hands, in His creation. God is green in the trees, red in the roses, melodic in the voice of the birds. He is laughter. He is tears. He is a rainbow. He is life in its totality. A saint meets God in every person and in every thing.

A saint is a great lover of God and His creation. The saint's life is a passionate devotion to a living God. He does not find the burning love of God incompatible with the love for God's creatures. He has a vibrantly rich emotional life. He has human feelings and boiling, passionate blood. He is of the nature of divine fire. He is not attached to things. He is for God alone. But the spouse, the child, the neighbor, the tree, the bird – each of these is part of the One who is. After all, God is not one more thing or a replacement for something else. God is the all, the Alpha and the Omega.

A saint does not love God in a vacuum. A saint does not love God in her head only. A saint does not love God in a contemplative prayer only. A saint participates creatively in life. She cares. She considers herself to be one with any part of creation, as well as with the whole. Only by being one with them can they be redeemed. A saint cannot be saved alone. She is saved by saving others. She is an unparalleled example of wholeness. She is a living fire, full of emotions. She lives fully. She knows no pettiness, coldness, mediocrity, or apathy. Only this kind of person, a saint, knows how to commit herself unconditionally, with the powerful passionate love, to supreme values by realizing union with God. A saint lives her love for God passionately and intensely, and in doing does not need to draw narrow boundaries around her love, excluding creatures. There is no such thing as inadequate love or loving too much. There are only bad relationships that stem from insufficient love. They are either diverted or distorted by a sick ego.

This capacity for divine and human love, we can probably say, is the foundation for true sanctity. Must we risk our lives for the sake of others? Sanctity, our friendship with God, depends on the answer to this question. A real lover will go to the extreme. A saint can have defects – who can pretend to be perfect anyway? But a saint can never be apathetic. His God is not remote, somewhere in the sky, far, far away; He is a God of love, incarnate, in history, in process today. Creatures attract and delight a saint but never imprison him. The more he loves God, the more he loves creatures. Greed and lust are out of the question because a greedy and lustful person does not know how to truly love.

A saint is intense. A saint lives passionately, with an ardent zest for life. She lives an ordinary life but knows the secret for transforming the ordinary into the extraordinary. She sees the divine in every happening. She sees God in every person she meets. She dares enough to be different, "strange," wild enough to be led by the fire of love no matter what, humble enough to admit her human errors, real enough to make many of us appear phony and ridiculous, simple enough to be like an innocent child, transparent enough that her neighbor can taste the divine through him, adventurous enough that she attempts to give birth to the world by giving a new birth to a spouse, a child, a neighbor, courageous enough that she can challenge any structure, any institution, any human law – with God's grace and love.

Meeting a saint is threatening. Wherever he happens to be, values turn upside down. The citadels of lust, hatred, competitiveness, lying and any wrongdoing with which people tend to fortify themselves crumble before someone who is not afraid to love them. And all this is possible because a saint no longer lives by the old law that gave the precept of charity and mercy, but by the new law, which is based on the presence of the Holy Spirit in his heart, which gives him the power to do what otherwise would have been impossible. In spite of his obvious weaknesses, a saint does "impossible" things, precisely because of the grace given to him and because he allows the Holy Spirit to work through him. Perfection is never satisfaction with one's current condition. Perfection is not static. Holiness requires growth, like a seed. No matter how perfect a seed may seem, it is imperfect if it does not grow into a plant. Growth is the work of the Holy Spirit. Aware of this, the saint allows it to happen.

A saint is open to the Holy Spirit.

A saint is the greatest lover there is.

27

Are You Holy-Whole?

To be holy is to be whole. A saint is not perfect – a saint is totally human.

Being perfect means that you have chosen already one side, and you have chosen to become fixed, frozen, not flowing. You become a "perfect" leftist, a "perfect" rightist, a "perfect" anything you choose to be. But life does not need anything perfect. With perfection, change would no longer be possible. Life needs the imperfection of change. Do not be afraid of being wrong, you're learning. If you are perfect, what is needed? You are, in a sense, dead. Wholeness and totality should be the goal, not perfection.

As I see it, a saint or any great man or woman is total, wholesome. Total means that they have everything in them with this in mind, that they are not the arithmetical total of everything, but rather the artistic total. A symphony is not the arithmetical total of the playing notes. A poem is not the arithmetical total of the words. In art, certain harmonies arise that are beyond what we see, hear, read, beyond the total that this particular piece of art has in form.

When you are whole, total, you have all the notes in you, from the far right to the far left – all the colors, like a rainbow. But you are not the sum of these different colors. You are the dynamic harmony of them, in tune with them. And this is the beauty of it. You remain constantly fresh, young, green, never flat, never boring, always vibrant, celebrating the joy of being alive.

Try to define Jesus. Can you? Was he conservative, progressive, rightist, leftist, too religious, not religious enough, pro-Roman, anti-Roman, with Moses, against Moses? You can never put Jesus in a category. He is total. He has it all. He is the harmony of all the colors together. That is why He is always fresh, always inspiring, always dynamic, always young, always new, always here and now.

It is easier to be perfect than to be total. Somehow, we are afraid of totality; we may not be able to handle it. Our minds prefer perfection because they understand it. Our minds like to be "perfectionist," and all our educational systems prepare us and train us in that direction. On the one hand, to be perfect, we have to choose. The more specific your choice is, the more perfect you become. You will know every detail concerning what you have decided to choose. And in the other hand, when you choose, you become partial, you drop all other possibilities. If you choose to be a mathematician, you may drop the possibility of being a painter or a poet. If you choose it to be intellectually regimented, you drop the possibility of being spontaneous. In either case – when you choose to be more perfect or when you choose to drop the other possibility – your ego is involved. Ego loves perfection. Perfection, socially speaking, is more successful.

But totality is not easy. A total person is a mysterious person. He lives the harmony of the opposites. She is the rainbow. Imagine how he can be wise in his spontaneity or free in his wisdom. Imagine how she may know everything, yet look so simple. Imagine how sophisticated he may be and how down to earth. Imagine how complex she looks and how innocent and perhaps naive. Imagine how close she is to God and how far he still considers himself from that. Did you get the picture? Do you think love, if it is not total in the sense of a wise spontaneity, is worthwhile? I do not think a perfectionist can really love. Only a total person can love.

And totality is difficult in another sense also. The more total you are, the more difficult you are to be understood by others. You become like a forest with no maps, no plans, no rules, just wild growth. Unpredictable. No symmetry. No logic. Picture Jesus before you. A mixture of divinity and flesh. The most profound wisdom the earth has ever seen and the greatest madness that has never happened before in the world. The Prince of Peace and yet the most passionate radical fighter of ideas. An oasis and yet divine fire, alive. Here is the beauty of Jesus. He attracts you so much, intrigues you, and he scares you too. He is all. He is the harmony of the all. He is not "perfect." He is "total." And the more total a person is, the more he becomes like God. The more whole, the more holy.

You depend on the whole after all, and the whole depends on you too. There is no separatedness whatsoever. There is only interdependence. We are part of a cosmic net. Nothing is unrelated. The whole is an organic unity. Only when the inordinate ego, the byproduct of human ignorance, intervenes, problems arise. That ego is the effort to prove to yourself that you are disconnected from the whole. Then you are in hell. You lose your meanings in life. You feel futile, unneeded, useless because you are uprooted, ungrounded. Then wars start within and without. Divisions are false at the center. They are only meaningful at the periphery, when your utilitarian "you" intervenes. In reality, the whole has no boundaries. Life is unity, but the ego divides. Do not create conflict within you in the first place. Do not discard anything God has given you. Use everything according to His holy plan. You are beautiful as you are. Live totally, intensely. Never pass a flower without deep concern and care in your heart. You make the flower bloom, and it returns your blessing with happiness in your heart. Only in the whole – in the harmony of the interdependent state – can you relax. The perfect person has division and tension in him. The total person is one, has no tension. He cannot make harmony with a simple note. He needs all the notes. There is no political, no sacred, no profane, no morality, no "religion," no philosophy, no economics – and yet there are all of them together. There is life. There is God. Only through totality may you be able to transcend. Only through totality will you understand all that you are doing, give meaning to your own life, and be able to be transformed in the process.

A whole person need not compromise. She is open to both sides of truth together. She does not deny things. At a deeper level, when you deny one side of what reality is, you compromise with the other. In a sense, it seems that we cannot live without choosing. War or peace. Either/or. But the fact is that reality is a unity of contradictions. It is a dialectical movement. It is a harmony of the opposite notes. It cannot be solo. Trust the whole. The whole is the best way to be alive, to be holy.

A whole person is also passionate. He lives what he is doing totally and intensely. He is totally committed to it, fully involved in it, with all his consciousness and heart. Unholy is the one who lives in a fragmentary way, divided, desintegrated, half-heartedly. A whole person is total, passionate, holy. The glory of God becomes manifest when one is fully alive, when matter is so spiritual, so dynamic, and when spirit is so incarnated, so concrete that you can no more tell what it is! "This is my beloved son on whom my favor rests. Listen to him" (Matthew 17:5).

When you become richer in every dimension of your being, you will be able to share more. And the more you share, the richer you become because you become more loving, more meditative, more creative. You'll give with gratitude, and you'll receive with generosity. You'll accept reality. What is whole is holy and what is holy is whole. Holy whole!

ℰꙮ

2 8

On Religion

Upon entering into the world as a human being, you are
nurtured as a Jew, a Christian, a Muslim, a Hindu, a
Buddhist, among countless other traditions. Your heritage
and conditioning come first, or you don't know who you
really are. Religion is not politics. In politics, you use everything, religion included, for your own interests. In religion,
you free yourself from everything, politics included. You
free yourself from others, and you free others from yourself.
Religion sets you free, especially from the God you have
"created."

When you think about God, it is usually philosophy,
theology, metaphysics, history, social and psychological
studies – just scientific speculation. Only when you live God
does religion start to make sense. When you look at a
flower and you think about it, you are puttering in science,
and perhaps in aesthetics or philosophy. But when you
look at the flower with pure eyes, as God's creation, without
the contamination of thought, and you experience the beauty
of that flower, you are participating in the mystery of existence. Then there is somehow a communion with the
flower. Boundaries are lost. You feel the essence of the
flower within you, and you become, in a sense, the flower.

Religion is real when it becomes your every experience. You don't borrow knowledge or belief; you personally witness God, you live God. And if you feel solidarity with others, your solidarity is not a simple support from and for your own community; it is a solidarity with existence itself and with God. Your solidarity becomes creativity, participation in God's work, religion. You will feel also that you are not really the doer, but an instrument of God. God is the real doer. God flows through you. Then great things begin to happen. Your beliefs, traditions, and ethics will not make you a person of religion. Does the language you speak make you a good citizen of the country you happen to be in?! You re a person of religion when you become a simple flute for the lips of God and you allow Him to play His songs through you.

Religion is not what you do for God: sacrifice, fasting, mortification, prayer. Religion is the realization of the great things that God has done for you. The miracles of life that we will never know to a sufficient degree. Why do we keep living with this view of ourselves as lordly benefactors, benefactors even to God Himself?

Religion is essentially a rebellion, not conformity. Conformity is something mechanical. You do what you are expected to do. You don't want problems within the group you belong to, do you? Your need to belong to an organization, a society, a church compels you to follow the rules. You are afraid to be alone, isolated, lonely. You follow what you see. You conform yourself to the past, to traditions created by people who are not there anymore. And you start to behave as if you were following Jesus, Buddha, or Muhammed. Your signature is there, but you are not there. Religion is not intoxication. Religion gives awareness. This awareness urges rebellion because religion deals with truths, not incidentals. Incidentals are temporary. Truths are eternal. You can learn incidental facts in books. You cannot learn truths except by living them. Religion is not an argument, a proof, or a theology. Religion is a type of trust, and it cannot be otherwise. Religion is not a fiction, an abstraction, a mere word. Religion is concerned with concrete existence. What does love of humanity mean if you are not able to love another human being? Humanity is nowhere. You never meet "humanity," you come across a particular human beings. To say that you love humanity is easy because you need not love any specific individual. But it is not easy to love your neighbor as yourself. Your religious life should consist of loving your wife, your husband, your children, your next-door neighbors, your work. Do you think you are closer to God than you are to your neighbor or to your work?

To think that we have a meaningless life means that we have a meaningless God. The true atheist is the one who says not that God does not exist, but that God cannot be present in his daily life and therefore cannot change him. The true atheist always seeks God in any other way than the Incarnation. Don't you read the gospel? The Transcendent is someone who washes our feet. And to Peter, or to you, or to me, or to anyone else who may be scandalized by this notion, Jesus would say, "If I do not wash you, you will have no share in my heritage" (John 13:8). The transcendent has flesh and bones. "If anyone says, 'My love is fixed on God,' yet hates his brother, he is a liar. One who has no love for the brother he has seen cannot love the God he has not seen" (1 John 4:20). Religion is neither history nor tradition nor fiction. Religion deals with the here and now. That is why no status quo will find its place in true religion. Truth is beyond masks of personalities and beyond incidentals. Religion is rebellion. It is a continuous attempt to give birth to a living God in this continuously changing world of ours.

Religion is not merely a psychological, sociological, or spiritual consolation. Religion challenges you, keeps you in a continuous storm. God will never stop stirring you with the inspirations of the Spirit. You don't feel at rest in any place or any time. "Traditional" religions console you by helping you to hide your wounds. It is not in their interest to let you be true to yourself or let you dare to be adventurous. You go to church to feel "at peace" with God, others, and yourself, and in doing so you become a respected person. To become a member of a church certainly helps. People think you are religious. In addition, you will feel relieved as a result of speaking to God about your problems. And if the situation remains the same, you will feel consoled because you did what you had to do: pray. Religion is much more than simple consolation. Religion gives you a new consciousness. It is a new being arising from within. This new consciousness brings new eyes, new looks, new ways of seeing things. Not that your problems are necessarily solved. They are simply dissolved. They disappear. Your new vision encompasses much more than your tiny problems. Religion is not a "tranquilizer." Your rituals are not medicines or drugs you take to escape the difficulties of life. Religion is the path to the actualization of all your potentialities. Aren't you created in the image of God? Difficulties will certainly arise, but they become opportunities instead of obstacles in your endeavor to know God. They become your way to God, rather than obstacles that get in the way of your relationship with God.

The religion that creates invisible chains to bind your soul is a dangerous religion. It can kill your soul. "Do not fear those who deprive the body of life but cannot destroy the soul. Rather, fear him who can destroy both body and soul in Gehenna" (Matthew 10:28). Slavery has changed form. It has become more sophisticated. When you chain the body, the spirit still goes free. But when you chain the spirit, you commit the worst of crimes. To make every person feel guilty is the greatest strategy for enslaving the person and destroying his or her dignity. True religion does not enslave you. It liberates you. Its laws do not place limitations on your potentialities. They are rather indications of a greater fulfillment for your personality. Religion is a reverence for life. Religion gives life even to inanimate objects. Whatever religion touches becomes alive, since religion pours into it a magical meaning, and that makes all the difference in the world.

Religion is not the capacity to give our intellectual assent to dogma or to authoritatively declared truths. Religion is not abstractions. God does not want to be isolated in a remote heaven. God wants to be involved in life here and now. He does not want to be reduced to a God made of words, good feelings, and reassuring slogans. Such a "god" can become, without our knowledge, a substitute for the God of faith who wants a deep encounter with our inner self. It is possible to protect ourselves from the fire of God with even the most religious of "items." Religion is a dynamic mode of living. It is a conversion of our whole being by a total surrendering to God. It is a fundamental change of heart. It is a transformation from the old self to the new one. It is a new identity in God. That is why belonging to religion is different, very different, from belonging to a party or to a club. For in religion, you go much further. God's breath, His very Self, becomes your breath and your way and style of life. Your hands become God's hands. Your face becomes God's face. Your eyes become God's eyes. Everything may remain the same, and yet everything about you will change because you have been changed by your Redeemer through love.

True religion will effect in you a radical change.

ॐ

29

This Is Freedom

Only in true freedom can one flower. Freedom is probably the soul's deepest need.

All of human history is the history of freedom. Hegel put it this way: "The history of the world is none other than the progress of the consciousness of freedom." There are thousands and thousands of slaveries and people fighting for liberation. When you become free politically, the struggle does not cease. Only one type of slavery has been eliminated. But when you become free politically, you become more aware of other types of slaveries. And so, the struggle continues.

True freedom is not political, economic, social, psychological, or religious. It is not the license to say whatever you want to say without censure. Even if all these are important aspects of freedom, they still do not equal true freedom. True freedom is a spiritual phenomenon. It has something to do with your innermost being. It is an existential truth. Political freedom is good in itself, as are wonderful economic freedoms, social freedoms, psychological freedoms, and religious freedoms. But none of these come close to spiritual freedom – freedom from things, objects, and oneself; freedom from being possessed by anything.

Detachment is freedom!

Any kind of freedom, except spiritual freedom, can be taken away. Is freedom that can be snatched away from you really freedom?

A spiritual freedom cannot be chained. It cannot be held in jail. True freedom remains true, even in chains and even in jail. Nobody can take your true freedom from you except you.

Do we really know what we are? We have been taught and trained to conform to the ways of others so thoroughly that we may not know what is our own way and what we want. Our parents, teachers, friends, books, TV, etc. . . . are there to help us make the "right" decision. They even make the decision for us. And we pretend to be free. Freedom is freedom from one's false self in the first place. Freedom from the various social roles we usually identify ourselves with. Freedom from our programming – that collection of desires, motivations, expectations, ideals, and demands on which our ego focuses most of our energy. Freedom from the "somebody" we strive to become. Freedom from the addictions and patterns we have unknowingly programmed as the path to our happiness. Freedom from the thoughts, ideas, opinions, and words that result from this programming. Freedom from our cherished notions, concepts, and assumptions. Freedom from our very self. Isn't this the meaning of one of Jesus' most penetrating sayings: "Whoever wishes to be my follower must deny his very self. . . . Whoever would save his life will lose it, and whoever loses his life for my sake will save it" (Luke 9:23-24). In a sense, the less cultivated we are, the more real we become. The less idealistic we are, the more honest and authentic.

The most essential thing is not to make the self free, but to be free from the self. The seed, to grow, must lose itself as seed. Otherwise no growth is possible.

When you reach your innermost center, your ego loses ground. You are no more. The social factor that makes you what you think you are fades away. You would act from your heart, not from your personality. Your attitude becomes authentic, not a mere formality, a label, an etiquette. And when you say something, you mean it. "Say, 'Yes' when you mean 'Yes' and 'No' when you mean 'No'" (Matthew 5:37). You are free. It is a wonderful experience to live without a personality mask. You are freed from your own personality.

But this freedom has a price; freedom is never "free." Each moment of freedom is full of dangers – you may fall – but also full of possibilities. You may enjoy all kinds of growth. There are always risks. There is insecurity. There is the unknown. There is a possibility for error. But even to err, one has to be free, responsible and conscious. That is why one fears freedom. Slavery is somehow comfortable. Somebody else takes responsibility. With freedom, one has to make his or her own choices. Then the struggle begins, and also the chance for peace. With the collapse of conditionings and all kinds of prejudices, there is a chance for peace indeed. Freedom, this kind of freedom, is the path to real peace. It is the opposite of prejudice.

True freedom is therefore a spiritual matter. You can be bound by circumstances and still be free. But if you are bound inside and free in circumstances, you are not free. You can have all the money of the world, you can leave your job and travel wherever and whenever you want, and have whatever you desire (as many people do) but this does not make *you* free. The outer circumstances help but do not affect you. Don't get yourself caught in others' opinions, not even in your own opinions, because opinions give substance to your belief. And if opinions crumble, you will be totally confused.

Stay alert. Remain free. As a slave, you cannot reach God. Freedom is difficult, but true freedom is the real joy for human beings. It is the most challenging and appealing path to God. You can see God in freedom only when you start peeling away your true self's masks until you reach the core of your being. God is right there. He is the essence of your being. Be free and see.

၆၁

30

Jesus' Strategy

The Scribes and the Pharisees – the learned people –
brought to Jesus a woman taken in adultery.

They were not concerned with the woman, even
though, in a sense, they were. They were not concerned
with Moses himself, even though, in a sense, they were.
They were not concerned with Jesus as somebody you can
learn from, or somebody you can share with, or somebody
in whose consciousness you can participate. No. They were
concerned with the trap.

They said to Jesus, "Teacher, this woman has been
caught in the act of adultery. In the law, Moses ordered
such women to be stoned. What do you have to say about
the case?" (John 8:4-5).

Their definition of adultery is clearly legalistic and has
nothing to do with the human heart, love, or consciousness.
It has nothing to do with depth. The woman's behavior is
sinful because it goes directly against what was said in the
book. But what about the man who was with her? Can she
be caught in adultery alone? Nothing is said about the man.

It was a puzzling situation, indeed! Jesus had to find
a way out without saying anything against Moses, and yet
He did not want to apply or negate the law. The wondrous

answer came this way: "Let the man among you who has no sin be the first to cast a stone at her" (John 8:7). Immense intelligence, wisdom, compassion, and awareness!

And Jesus stooped down to allow them freedom to think about this and remember, and to give them a chance to escape if they wanted to do so, which is precisely what they chose to do. Then Jesus said, "Woman, . . . has no one condemned you? . . . Nor do I condemn you. You may go. But from now on, avoid this sin" (John 8:10-11).

Jesus converted the accusers. He suggested a one hundred eighty degree turn. From the woman to themselves, He redirected the question. From the law to their consciousness, He diverted their minds. They became their own targets. The law is important. But there is something more important than the law.

The moralist always finds something that does not correspond to what is written in the book. He always accuses, he always condemns. The deeply spiritual person always approaches with a different attitude, the attitude of acceptance and forgiveness. The past is gone. We learn lessons from it and try not to make the same mistakes again.

Jesus transformed people through His forgiveness. This was one of the greatest accusations against Him. "Who is this man who utters blasphemies? Who can forgive sins but God alone?" (Luke 5:21). But that feeling of well being, which comes from shaking off the past and getting on with the present, contains something of a miracle, does it not? It gives courage, enthusiasm, and freshness, and it opens new doors and new possibilities. You feel alive and new and free once again. You feel loved. God loves you. And you make a fresh start.

Jesus alone sees people as they really are. He sees deep into the heart of each one of us. He is completely aware of what is going on, even in the inner core of our consciousness. That is why he was rather tolerant of prostitutes, thieves, the sick, drunkards, ordinary people. But he was tough with the "pious." For these he reserved epithets such as "hypocrites," "blind guides," "fools," "whitewashed tombs," "lawless serpents," "brood of vipers," and "murderers" because they performed pious duties and obeyed the Mosaic law in all its detail, while neglecting to cleanse their interior lives of their own wrongs and intemperance and failing to demand justice and mercy for their fellow human beings.

Jesus defended Mary Magdalene against everyone – Judas, Martha, and especially Simon, the Pharisee who invited Him to dinner. Everyone in town thought of Simon as a just man, a saint, and of Mary Magdalene as a sinner. Jesus said to Simon, "You see this woman? I came to your home and you provided me with no water for my feet. She has washed my feet with her tears and wiped them with her hair. You gave me no kiss, but she has not ceased kissing my feet since I entered. You did not anoint my head with oil, but she has anointed my feet with perfume. I tell you, that is why her many sins are forgiven – because of her great love. Little is forgiven the one whose love is small" (Luke 7:44-46).

Jesus, because He went straight to the heart of the matter without paying attention to the superficial, turned things upside down and declared a new order: "I assure you that tax collectors and prostitutes are entering the Kingdom of God before you" (Matthew 21:31). "The last shall be first and the first shall be last" (Matthew 20:16). Jesus was not suggesting reform for its own sake. Nor was He denying the religious and legal traditions of His people. He wanted to show that religion, tradition, and politics have to exist for the good of human beings, not vice versa. He wanted to show that a human being is more important than the stone temple. And that is why Jesus' strategy was to call humankind to life rather than to any particular religious acts. And that is why He always tried to free people from guilt. Even on the cross, His last words were, "Father, forgive them; they do not know what they are doing" (Luke 23:34).

Forgiveness, not guilt, was Jesus' strategy. Guilt paralyzes, drains the self of motivations, absorbs all energy. Guilt is a device used to control oneself and especially others. The guilt system is useful for society. It makes things work. Everybody has to follow the law, or become a criminal. It is even safe to say that the lives of individuals, as well as civilization itself, are impossible without the function of guilt. But we have to admit that it is one thing to emphasize this function, as our Judeo-Christian civilization has done, and quite another to consider guilt as a starting point for a new life by allowing freedom and responsibility, as Jesus did. Jesus, by paying attention to the deep insights and needs of all people, was the liberator who restored and developed people's self-worth. He didn't care about the social order and conventions. He could talk with the woman of Samaria. He could be a guest in the home of Zacchaeus. He could forgive the woman who was caught in adultery. When Jesus entered a house, it became a temple. When Jesus spoke to someone, that person became sacred, also a temple of the divine.

Forgiveness, not guilt, is the real moral act and the real political act. Forgiveness is love. Guilt is not love. Forgiveness allows life and truth to emerge anew. Forgiveness is the highest form of love.

Our society is built somewhat on the notion that "you must have done something wrong." We have convinced ourselves that we are sinners. Preachers make a big deal of our sins. Teachers remind us all the time of this "truth." Priests convey the message that if we don't feel guilty, we aren't on our way to heaven.

This scenario could be a good way to prevent disasters. It could even be a "religious" way. But it is surely not Jesus' way. Jesus' way is the way; forget about false guilt. Jesus forgave; just forgive.

When you put aside that false guilt and you decide to forgive others and yourself, miracles may happen to all. Remember, there was a resurrection as well as a cross.

୫ଠ

31

Paradoxical Jesus

Jesus was a paradox. He was intriguing, contradictory, and unpredictable. He created chaos. And worse, He enjoyed this chaos. He was a-moral, I mean, He did not follow the rules of His society. His morality was new. It was from within. He was spontaneous. He lived with the here-and-now approach. He appreciated each moment. He did not carry conclusions from the past. Except to conform to the will of His Father, He did not have a defined agenda. He had no clear map for how to live either. He would simply be there, reacting to each situation in a different loving way. His response was always fresh. That is why there are so many contradictions in His words. One day He would say, "Peace is my farewell to you, my peace is my gift to you" (John 14:27). Then He said, "Do not suppose that my mission on earth is to spread peace. My mission is to spread, not peace, but division" (Matthew 10:34). Another day He would say, when you want to pray, "Go to your room, close your door, and pray to your Father in private" (Matthew 6:6). Then He would pray in the open with his disciples, "Our Father in heaven, hallowed by your name, your Kingdom come" (Matthew 6:9-10). Here He says, "Do not think that I have come to abolish the law and prophets. I have come, not to abolish them, but to fulfill them" (Matthew 5:17). And there He says, "The Sabbath was made for man, not man for the Sabbath" (Mark 2:27). And He would heal someone without any consideration to the regulations usually adhered to.

In other words, Jesus was full of contradictions. He was inconsistent and illogical. Do not even try to be logical with Jesus – you will miss Him. Try to understand Him through intuitions, not logic. What He says is not an argument or a proof of something. It is simply a declaration of truth. His language is the language of a lover, full of poetry, filled with love, zest, enthusiasm, exaggerations, craziness. You cannot follow Jesus without going joyfully crazy. He was so vast that He contained all contradictions, all polarities, like life itself.

Jesus Christ was Jesus and Christ. He is the meeting point where two worlds meet, Christhood and humanhood, infinite and finite, divine and human, spiritual and material. Jesus was the unity, and in the unity there is no duality. Hence the ecstasy of Jesus.

Christian ideology pictured Jesus as a sad man, almost always associated with the cross. That is only a caricature of Him. Jesus must have been ecstatically joyful. He must have been overflowing with joy and great delight. How could He have been otherwise? When the opposites meet, there is ecstasy. When there is unity between the sacred and the profane, there is ecstasy. There is also ecstasy when the water merges with the sun, the earth with the sky, the body with the soul, the heart with the brain, matter with spirit. Jesus is the synthesis of the opposites. That is why He looks, on the surface, so contradictory. All depends on how you look at Him and/or what you need to see. Jesus reveals you to yourself. He would reflect your own contradictions. In Him, the polarities have disappeared. Dualism disappeared. He can even say, for example, "The

Father and I are one" (John 10:30). But the Jewish tradition failed to understand this. One of the reasons for His crucifixion was that He transgressed this concept of dualism. Only when you are able to go beyond any dualistic point of view can you start to feel the sacredness of everything, and then you start to celebrate life. Exactly as Jesus did. Jesus never divided the ordinary life from the spiritual life. Jesus enjoyed life. Life is a gift from God. When you learn to enjoy this gift, you express your gratitude to God and you become capable of enjoying of God. But again, some Christians preferred to choose the unhappy moments of Jesus' life only, and they created places to practice all kinds of asceticism in order to imitate Him. Masochism and self-tortures became dominant, and the feasting of Jesus disappeared. This was their way of looking at Jesus. But Jesus was total, whole, a synthesis of divinity and humanity. He loved life. He loved the world.

Shouldn't we be as paradoxical as Jesus was and love everything that God has given to us according to His plans for us? Shouldn't we love this world and contribute to its evolution toward divinity? A follower of Jesus is, like Jesus, a walking paradox too.

ॐ

32

They Are Afraid of a Living Jesus – Are You?

It seems safe enough to say that Christianity, as the structured institution we know it, was not founded by Jesus.
Christianity was and is founded mainly by those who "crucified" Him and continue to "crucify" Him.

Once the Master is gone, politics enters the scene.
Followers start fighting about who is the greatest disciple,
who is the successor, who is right and who is wrong, who
should be in the Kingdom of God and who should be
excluded from it. That is why we see a thousand and one
divisions, some caused by foolish things, not even worthy
to be mentioned. Who is going to believe that all these
denominations were created for the sake of pluralism and
the common good of the people of God? It is very difficult
for the temple to remain a temple when the holy of holies
is missing. When the shepherd is gone, wolves appear
between the sheep.

Christianity, at least in its sociological face, is created
by the same type of people who crucified Jesus. The people
who crucified and continue to crucify Jesus are the high
priests, the phony politicians, the money-hungry businesspersons, the Judas, the hypocrite, the Pharisees, the power

seekers, the liars. Of course, religion is of a great interest to these people. They can transform religion into a source of income, power, and prestige. These people have interest in religion, but no interest in Jesus because He won't listen to them. They are afraid of the living Jesus. At His death, they can gather and create a structure, a ritual, an institution. They try to improve upon the original face of Jesus, as Christianity did throughout the centuries. Then you can go to the temple, the cathedral, and all kinds of churches, and you can enter into rituals, sometimes just to escape the real Jesus. It is safe to do rituals. It is risky to meet the real face of Jesus. Imagine what would happen if we peeled off all the paint that covered the original face of the Master. Who, among all those who are crucifying Him, dares to face *the truth, and the way, and the life?* (John 14:6). Who needs this fire? Jesus proved that He can make a big mess. He did it one time when He wanted to cleanse the temple (John 2:13-17; Matthew 21:12-13; Mark 11:15-16; Luke 19:45-46).

The sharpest critic of formal religion is Jesus Himself. He wanted people to live religious lives, not just speculate about religion or make of it a mere institution and a well-structured edifice. He never listed rules. He did not say a word about contemplation and cloisters. He was not concerned with the hierarchy as such. He was not interested in who should be first and who should be second. He preferred to communicate to His disciples the gift of love, His Spirit, which was to lead them and teach them His truth. At His resurrection, He did not destroy the stone of His tomb only, but He abolished all the barriers that used to keep us in our prisons: classes, races, languages, nationalities, times, places, distances, and even genders. "There does not exist among you Jew or Greek, slave or freeman, male or female. All are one in Christ Jesus" (Galatians

3:28). He even abolished the distance between this world and the beyond.

There is a rebellion in Christ. Rebellion cannot be organized. You will kill it the moment you organize it. Jesus is above all churches and institutions and structures. All the structures of society are insignificant next to Christ: capitalism, Marxism, class, privilege, racial distinctions, wealth, education and culture, and even religion and spirituality. Jesus was not among those who enjoyed privileges. Christ was universal, not "Christian." It is scary to fall in the hands of a living God. He does not want a sociological religion. Many Christians – even though they practice the established religion that they learned and that has all the answers past, present, and future – are not really living Christians. These are not interested in Jesus Himself. Their whole interest is in how to protect themselves from illness, bankruptcy, breakdown, death, and loss of power and privilege. And this exactly was what Jesus did not want. So it is better for them not to have to deal with the living Jesus.

In true religion, Jesus is alive. If Jesus is not alive in a religion, this religion is simply an institution, even though it might be a successful institution. Harmony with the state, the society, and private lifestyles is not more important than the identification with Christ. Are we all that we can be? Are we all that we should be? Jesus asks for a totally new way of thinking and living, a revolution in our consciousness, both private and public. A radical change in our attitude and behavior. A new order that is based on the assertion that "no man can serve two masters" (Matthew 6:24), and on breaking out of the group and opening up to others and washing their feet, on forgiveness, compassion, vulnerability, and communion with one another. The new order appeared so clearly at the Last Supper! Here Jesus overturned the whole social order and gave His disciples a taste of a real, living community. He did not respect the conventions. He never did. He went against the systems, the arguments, the logics, the organizations, the status quo. He taught new insights for life and love. He lived new truths and new ways. He made things alive in new appreciation never before heard of.

Christianity does not always converge with what Jesus really was in life. Yet He must be the measure for all things. Other measures are questionable, inconsistent, and unreliable.

Try the living, flesh-and-blood Christ, for He is right here. Now. He is no farther away than your closest neighbor. He dwells within your community – in the *communion.* "Where two or three are gathered in my name, there am I in their midst" (Matthew 18:20).

Try it.

Just try this and see the difference. Do not be afraid!

ജ

33

When Their Abstractions Contribute to Our Problems

Have you ever met an abstract thinker who is happy, satisfied, and contented?

Science gives us answers. Religion gives us answers. What answers do mere abstractions give us? All their answers are beautiful facades that hide, most of the time, frustrations, depressions, or at least dissatisfactions. Deep down, abstract thinkers, like so many philosophers, for example, bring more questions to us than answers. Every answer that abstract philosophy gives leads to more questions. Has abstract philosophy solved any problem so far?

A system may convince you of something. However, it does not convert you. There is no flame within it.

Abstract thinkers have been thinking for centuries and trying to explain all in life through theories. But life does not follow their logic. Life is not a collection of theories. Reality is not a system. Abstract thinking is a labyrinth or a maze that leads to nowhere. Truth liberates us, not theories. Words, knowledge, logical systems do not touch your soul. Truth is not found in what you know, what you have, or what you do. Truth is found in who and what *you are*. You cannot find it. You are it.

With abstract thinking, one becomes intellectual. Very intellectual. And the more intellectual one becomes, the less understanding one is. Life cannot be limited to its intellectual aspect. Life has its own laws and principles. They are not necessarily yours. Life does not follow your principles.

With abstract thinking, one accumulates knowledge – the kind of knowledge that goes around and around. An abstract philosopher, for example, never knows directly. Her knowledge is not a direct penetration in the mystery of life. She can never know the way the seed knows how to grow and the bud knows how to open in the early sun. A philosopher may know a lot about God, but have you ever heard about a philosopher becoming a saint? There are saints who were philosophers, but not because of their philosophy. Philosophy, even if it may help in some way, is not the best way of knowing God, and especially of becoming religious. Sainthood needs another kind of intelligence.

The irony here is that when a person is too well-informed and too knowledgeable – as an abstract thinker usually is – his very knowledge becomes the barrier that prevents him from seeing the profound truth. He builds a thick wall of words to rely upon for protection. He does not want any surprise in his life. A surprise is not included in the system. It is not logical. But life is filled with constant surprises. The ordinary life is so extraordinary because God comes always in small incidents – a child smiling, a dog barking, a flower blooming, a bird singing. It is so difficult for an abstract thinker to see God there because his view is blocked by so much knowledge. Scholars in general and philosophers in particular, and maybe theologians too, cannot see what is before their eyes and cannot hear what is being said. They are full of their own ideas, and reality cannot reach their hearts. To these people, more than to the crowd, Jesus says, "They look but do not see, they listen but do not hear or understand" (Matthew 13:13).

Jesus never liked the company of the scholars and the priests of that time. He was even very harsh toward them, saying, "I assure you that tax collectors and prostitutes are entering the Kingdom of God before you" (Matthew 21:31). For this these scholars, the word "God" becomes more important than what the word represents, and the word "love" becomes more important than what the word is trying to say. They miss the real thing while standing ready to kill each other over the word.

No one can get to the truth through successful debates, and a fortiori through victorious, bloody battles. In this context, most literate people are corrupted. Do you know any essential question that has been solved by a theoretical system? No system is true when dealing with reality. In real life, you open your eyes and you see, you open your ears and you hear, you meet someone in need and you help him or her, you visit a prisoner, you keep company with an elderly person, you comfort a sick person, you cook a meal for a hungry person, and you give a good shirt to someone who cannot afford to buy one. Only innocent and childlike people can detect the voice of the beyond.

Jesus was a concrete reality. People saw Him. They heard Him. They touched Him. And maybe that is why they crucified Him. He was not the Christ of their expectations, Scriptures, and theories.

We still are in the same situation. More books are written about Jesus than about anyone else, yet no one is as unknown as He is.

He is here and now, but we keep looking elsewhere. He is in our neighbor, and we prefer to "see" Him rather in an impeccable theory.

Our "beautiful theories" can, very often, contribute to our problems. Sometimes, they are our problems.

ॐ

34

A Loving Heart Beats in Tune with God's Heart

Very often, people think that it is of primary importance to think of God. It is, indeed. Maybe just to start. But do not come to a stop there. Saint Teresa of Avila used to say, "The important thing is not to think much, but to love much."

In fact, revelation is not just knowledge, nor it is a result of a logical system. Revelation is a kind of impulse that touches your heart and brings transformation.

For some reason, the sooner you get away from your head – at least when you pray – the more satisfaction and enjoyment you find. This is probably because you feel the living breath of God in your soul, in the present.

If you live only through your head, you are always living in the past or in the future. Regretting and feeling guilty about things in the past, or anticipating and dreaming of things in the future. To remember and to plan are important. But being in the present and living each moment will make you more alive.

In order to be in the present, what you can possibly do is to return to your senses. Perceive. Feel. See. Smell. Hear. Taste. Touch. Listen.

Feel the heat, the cold, the breeze. Feel the atmosphere, the ambiance, the environment. Let your skin touch
a leaf. Smell a rose. Taste an orange. Listen to "The Four
Seasons." Look at the full, smiling moon and whatever stars
you can see around it. Feel your heart beating and giving
meaning to all these beautiful things and to life itself. Medi-
tate deeply and often. Contemplation is not a fruit of your
head. Prayer is not a collection of words. So why you do
not move to intuiting, sensing, feeling, and loving? This is
the area where prayer becomes transforming power. Do
you know any saint who became a saint by just following
a coherent system, pursuing a logical deduction, or counting
on words and rites only? I don't. Saints love! A loving heart
beats in tune with God's heart.

ℬ

35

Surrendering to the Miracle of Love

Surrendering to love is not weakness. When you surrender to love, you prove your capability and your might.

In surrendering, you give up the intellect's control, but you do not lose your power. On the contrary, you confirm your own power of humanity. By being so vulnerable, so open and willing to receive, you take in more love, more freedom, and more of God.

Only love knows how to be "defeated." Who loves more, surrenders more. In love, to conquer is to lose. Your efforts and your continuous struggles create just the opposite of what you are looking for. These very efforts leave you in anguish and misery. Do not conquer love. Just surrender to it. Love will conquer you.

When you surrender to love, the entire universe surrenders to you. When you surrender to the whole, the whole returns your generosity multiplied. Strange economics! Miracle of love!

The very surrender of self transforms you much more than who or what you surrender to. The other is only an excuse, an opportunity for surrendering. You don't surrender to a vacuum. Except to God, the object of your surrendering is irrelevant. What is most important here is to put your ego aside and unburden yourself. In that very act of surrendering, your past disappears, and a new point comes into existence. Surrender creates a gap between you and your past, between you and your prejudices. Here, struggle is not needed. Not even will is needed. For surrender, the will rather becomes a problem. "You" will become a problem. That "you" is the basic problem. Any other problem is a byproduct. So put it aside. Why are you afraid? Why do you have to build walls around yourself? Do not count on defenses and aggressions of any kind. Just relax. Surrender is a total relaxation. It is a merging into the universe and the life that God has created. It is a reunion with God in such an intimate way that you feel you are no more. Only God is. You do not feel divisions. You do not feel boundaries. By disappearing, the waves become the ocean itself.

Yield, allow, cooperate, do not go against life's tides. Bow down. Give way. Participate in existence. Be whole. Relax. Live fully. Be totally alive. Let "you" go. Let God sing His song for you. Float in the river, and the river will take you to the ocean.

Surrender. When you totally surrender to God, your very act of surrendering will transform you. God will be in you, through you. Whatever you do, you will smell the same fragrance. Let be what God wills through you. Do not interfere. You will be always fresh, always original, and always unique; for you reflect the image of Him who is in you. The divine energy flows through all things, all time, all space. We need to open our ears and listen to it, rather than considering our superficial words to be the words of God. Fall in love with what is. Everything flows from the divine source. Just trust and surrender. Allow the breeze of God to flow through you. Then you will be able to perceive the deep meaning of Mary's words: "I am the servant of the Lord. Let it be done to me as you say" (Luke 1:38), and Paul's words: "The life I live now is not my own; Christ is living in me" (Galatians 2:20).

℘

36

Prayer Is Not a "Peaceful" Means

To be able to really pray, please put your head aside and focus on your heart.

You may want to start praying through thinking, learning, repeating certain formulas, understanding, even calculating, but don't stop there. If you do, sooner or later you will become frustrated and discouraged.

Move into the area of loving. Period. Here resides the power of transformation. For when you pray, you won't stay the same, and neither will the world. Prayer, in fact, is not intended to change God's mind about some incident or about some miracle we would like to see happen. In prayer, God makes us renounce our expectations to convert us to our surrendering to what is the best for us – Him. Prayer is intended to change us in the first place. And it takes time. That is why, for a good prayer, some time is required. An instant transformation does not happen so often. God's favorite prayer is the one that knows no interruption because God does not want to be the last resort in case of some accident. He wants to be with us at all times, and He does not want to give us less than Himself at any moment.

Prayer is an attitude of letting go of yourself. You open up to the Holy Spirit and let Him do His work in you. In prayer, you stop seeing things as you would like to see them. You start to see them as God sees them. A true prayer cannot be less than a total vulnerability to God, a surrender, a union, and an ecstasy.

Words are not an absolute requirement for prayer. As a matter of fact, when they are too long and burdened with traditions, words may lessen the effectiveness of prayer. We stop praying when we stop at the beautiful rituals without piercing beyond. In which case, words become barriers instead of bridges to the divine – goals instead of signs pointing toward the goal. Words are words. They are not real unless they are meaningful. God does not like mere words. He wants to be real, to incarnate. We pray only when we become what we say. Otherwise our prayer is not only a hypocrisy but also an apostasy. It is declaring that God is not capable of changing us. And it is also an idolatry, since we take the words of a prayer and we believe in them instead of what they represent. The Pharisee loves words and rituals and all the "shoulds." He is so "religious" that he thinks he does not have to be humane anymore. Instead of pulling him to the truth, his rites push him away from it. He can commit the worst atrocities in the name of religion and justify his actions in good conscience and faith. In the whole gospel, the only people Jesus could never tolerate were the Pharisees because they were liars and self-sufficient. Pharisees "like" God, whom they do not see, but do not like their brothers, whom they do see. They are "rich" with themselves, sure of their knowledge and satisfied with their practices. They want nothing to be changed, certainly not themselves. They don't allow themselves to be criticized by the Word of God, which they keep repeating with the calculation of their heads. Only a good prayer allows a person to be unsettled by God's word. Prayer is the death of an entire zone of ourselves in order to be born again in a completely new face.

Prayer is neither an illusion nor a place to which we can escape for security. When we pray the Our Father, for instance, are we aware that these two or three lines are also a practical program of action? When we go to church on Sunday, are we aware that our Christian life does not end in that church? Are we aware that this is where it begins? The church is not a bank where we can collect or deposit some good words for God, as a security measure, and maybe pay some insurance premium that allows us to benefit in the eternal life. At the Judgment, God won't ask us whether or not we said "Lord, Lord," or how many times we said it. The only question He is interested in is, What did we do for our brothers and sisters? Therefore, prayer is action. You really pray only when you integrate the two loves in your heart, love for God and love for others. In fact, it is the same love under different names. Jesus says that the second commandment is equal to the first one. So it is unreal to consider prayer as a contemplative feeling only. Prayer is also a participation in the world. Prayer is the incarnation of God, the indwelling of Him, in our lives. God has decided to need us. He did not want to do all the work alone. He gave us powers to participate in His continuous act of creation. Genuine contemplative prayer becomes active by reaching out to others. The person who is delighted in adding every day another formula of prayer to the fort of his cloister is a false contemplative. "I do not ask you to take them out of the world" (John 17:15). Prayer rectifies the illusions of action as action rectifies the illusions of "prayer." Prayer and action are not two separate things. Action is the expression of the love of God that we encounter in prayer. It is time to put an end to that phony opposition symbolized by Mary and Martha. The Old Testament already preaches the connection between the two, and it recommends pursuing justice instead of just fasting and offering sacrifices: "I hate, I spurn your feasts, I take no pleasure in your solemnities; your cereal offerings I will not accept, nor consider your stall-fed peace offerings. Away with your noisy songs! I will not listen to the melodies of your harps. But if you would offer me holocausts, then let justice surge like water, and goodness like an unfailing stream" (Amos 5:21-25), and "What care I for the number of your sacrifices? says the Lord. I have had enough of whole-burnt rams and fat of fatlings; in the blood of calves, lambs and goats I find no pleasure" (Isaiah 1:11; see also Isaiah 1:2; 58:1-9; Jeremiah 7:1-7; Joel 2:13).

With this in mind, do we realize how ridiculous appear the attitudes of those who read prayer books, the way invalids swallow drugs to relieve bodily pain? Prayer, even though it has a miraculous aspect, does not operate as medications do. Prayer operates from within. Its healing power is radical. It will change the old into new, all the time. With prayer, you grow young of heart and spirit.

Prayer is also opening our hands to the world in a sign of acceptance of all that surrounds us. The people we meet, the situations we are in, sufferings and joys tell the story of God in the human condition. God is real only in our own human condition. If we are sensitive enough to see Him right there, our life becomes a prayer, a continuous conversion. And when this does happen, we cannot help but have critical questions about the problems in the world. Even our life becomes itself a critical lifestyle for those who live otherwise. Who can stand the status quo after entering the reality of the Unseen! In this sense, prayer is not meant to be a "peaceful" means, but to turn things upside down and define again and again our top priorities and values. Prayer is a fundamental criticism for what it is. Never in a negative way, but always in a positive and constructive way. We really pray when we believe that we have a role to play in realizing the Kingdom of God. The more we pray, the more we become aware of the need for a new order, a new structure, a new quality of life. The praying person has a vision that inspires the world, a vision that invites others constantly to let go of their certainties and take the road again and again looking for fresh lands, new paths, and new avenues, and to expand a better living in a wider brotherhood and sisterhood. The praying person does not cease to pray. His prayer is not a part-time job. Whatever she happens to be doing becomes her prayer. There is no moment – walking, sitting, learning, eating, playing, listening, reading, waking, sleeping – that is not marked by the presence of God in him. Her whole life becomes living prayer. And "if you wish to know how such things come about, consult grace, not doctrine; desire, not understanding; prayerful groaning, not studious reading; the Spouse, not the teacher; God, not man; darkness, not clarity. Consult not light, but the fire that completely inflames the mind and carries it over to God in transports of fervor and blazes of love. This fire is God" (Bonaventure).

When you leave your head to move to your heart, you will understand all this, not by the way of thinking, but by the way of loving. And then you will really pray and experience the fire of God.

ဆ

3 7

When You Really Pray

When you really pray, you enter deeply into things, further than you would have first imagined. You convert yourself to a better understanding of self, your brothers and sisters in Christ, and, above all, your God. When you deepen your own understanding, you cannot help but ask critical questions about the conditions of the societal system you live in.

When you really pray, you declare that God is the only absolute, and everything else is only temporary and relative.

When you really pray, you declare your love and gratitude to your Creator, who gave you the power to cocreate with Him. Then you look forward to crafting a new self, a new environment, a new start, a new system, a new society, a new world. What you really want is something else. You seek change, expansion, your own transformation.

When you really pray, you can never rest and say, "This is it." You'll keep looking for a newer order, a newer structure, a newer life, a deeper relationship with your God.

When you really pray, you concentrate your eyes on the end of things, that is, on the infinite and the wholeness. And you keep growing and growing and growing. The Spirit is silently at work. The infinite and the wholeness are among His qualities. When you really pray, you have to expect to be silenced and persecuted, precisely because your attitude is a refusal of the values that make too many people feel secure. What would remain if these people were unmasked? Probably very little. They will try to get rid of you before you shake and threaten their tranquillity of mind. But your "death" is not in vain. The call for a new world becomes even louder.

When you really pray, you declare yourself ready to go further and further. Always afresh. With no preestablished certitudes. Prayer demands poverty of mind and openness of heart. You put a distance between yourself and things. And you enter into the reality of the Unseen. And you simply say, "Your kingdom come, your will be done on earth as it is in heaven" (Matthew 6:10).

When you pray, you put your feet in the steps of Jesus, like Simon who was forced to help to carry the cross. You fix your eyes on this One ahead. At that moment, you realize that something is moving. You are no longer the same after you have really prayed.

A revolution is not always a bloody one. But it is always a sweaty one.

Other kinds of prayers are only social duties, pleasant events an even empty religious phenomena.

ॐ

38

God Saw How Good It Was – Do You?

"God looked at everything he had made, and he found it very good" (Genesis 1:31). The world that God has made is therefore very good. To deny the goodness of the world is the matrix of many heresies.

God, human beings and nature are not rivals. They are not three disconnected realities separated by distinct boundaries. Human beings need not turn their backs on God in order to improve themselves. They need not despise what God has made in order to glorify Him.

In a sense, it is foolish to see God and what He has created as alternative poles, placed in a way that if we turn toward one we must turn our back to the other.

An "either/or" solution is unrealistic and simplistic, based on immaturity and prejudices. Human beings are united to God and also to the world. We share in both realities. We cannot live apart from either. Isn't this the meaning of the Incarnation of Jesus Christ, after all? The new humanity that can survive is precisely the one that can be reconciled and united to God and the world. "Both/and," not "either/or." To be aware of God in the world means to unite the divine and the human, the creator and the creation, the transcendent and the immanent, the spiritual and the material, the sacred and the profane, the religious and the scientific/technological, the subject and the object.

That idea of an antagonism between God and the world is not found in the Bible. Neither is it found in the early Fathers. Leave aside, for a while, all kinds of training and conditionings, and read with innocent eyes the psalms, for example, or Saint Irenaeus, or Saint Maximos the Confessor, or Saint Basil and his brother Gregory, or the mystics. You will see how the world is there to praise and glorify God, and how heaven and earth are worthy of equal honor. When you do, you will be surprised to see how shaky are the foundations of the dualistic theories, and also that part of the scholastic theology that is based on a static world system.

Our God is a person you can talk to, "our Father who is in heaven." He is also the reality around us. Listen to Meister Eckhart: "We must learn to penetrate things and find God there." Listen to Thomas Aquinas: "God is in all things and intimately so." Listen to Francis of Assisi: "All praise be yours, my Lord, through all that you have made, and first my Lord Brother Sun, who brings the day; and light you give us through him. . . . All praise be yours, my Lord, through Sister Moon and Stars. . . . All praise be yours, my Lord, through Sister Earth, our mother. . . ." God is not something hidden beyond the skies. He is the nearest immediate presence to you. He is also the possibility within you. He is a challenge, a risk, a danger, a mutation, a growth. He is what you are and what you are capable of becoming. He is the grace in you that forms the cornerstone of the spiritual and of the physical. Incarnation is the healing of dualism.

So welcome everything and enjoy it according to its original blessings from God. Enjoy the morning and the evening, the summer and the winter, spirit and body, life and death. Since the Incarnation, and since that day in which Jesus transformed the ordinary bread and wine into His Body and Blood, every ordinary thing has the potential to become a sacrament, and the entire earth a paradise again. Live the prayerful attitude of reconciliation. Prayer is not something abstract. It is something very practical. You cannot pray to God if you are not reconciled with your brother (Matthew 5:23-24) and with the world. How can you come to your Father, whom you do not see, if you do not talk to the brother you can see? How can you be reconciled with the unmanifest if you are not even capable of being reconciled with the manifest? The brother is not only that person you offended. The brother is also the sun, the stars, the trees, the animals, the rocks, the mountains, the water, yourself, your body, life, and existence itself. All of them are your brothers and sisters. Don't they come from the same source? Prayer is not only going to church and saying certain words. It is a bridge to a different consciousness, with an ecstatic peak that is not possible to attain unless if you are reconciled with what is. Prayer is a reconciliation, not a condemnation. How can you pray when you condemn what is – the world, others, and yourself, the nearest "other" to you? You really pray when you reconcile your soul with the soul of existence. When this happens, every little ordinary thing in life becomes sacramental. So why be condemning? Why not celebrate what God made and "saw how good it was"? When you reject yourself by condemning your body, for example, you are, in fact, taking a position against God, against God's body. Your body is His temple, his shrine; He has chosen to dwell in it. Take care of it. Make the best of it, in order to be ready to receive the Lord. Enjoy life through it, the way God wanted it to be enjoyed. Here and now, the body is not separate from the soul. Do you allow your right hand to fight with your left hand? Accept God and the world He has made.

This world is full of God. Wherever you walk, you walk on holy ground. Don't you see how one-sided are the traditions that want you to fight the world in order to reach the divine? They are as perverted as those that take the other extreme and indulge in empty pleasures. God is not beyond the world. He is at the very center of it. He is not like an author who writes a book and forgets about it. Rather, He is like a dancer. Can you separate a dance from a dancer? Don't exclude things. Include, integrate, grow, and expand. Look at the trees, the sky, the birds, your fellow men and women and include them all. Feel them within you. They are not your enemies. They are part of you, part of the whole. The Ultimate is hidden in their innermost. Absorb everything. A total "yes" is required from the one who believes in God. How can you accept the Creator while denying His creation? If you do so, you are putting yourself above God and deciding for yourself what is good and what is evil. You are repeating Adam and Eve's choice to eat from the forbidden tree. You are saying "no" to life. God is not only the beginning, He is also the end. Life is what happens between the beginning and the end. How can you reach the end without going through what is there, always evolving. The spiritual and the material attract each other. Our faith does not require us to throw away things of the earth, but rather to throw ourselves right into things of the earth. "Spirituality," says Meister Eckhart, "is not to be learned by flight from the world, by running away from things or by turning solitary and going apart from the world. Rather, one needs to learn an inner solitude, wherever or with whomever one may be. We must learn to penetrate things and find God there." The spiritual and the material are the two poles of one existence. Is there a river with one bank? The sin is not in the oneness of things. The real sin is in separating what is one already. Dualism is the sin, not oneness. Dualism is war. It kills. This is dualism that creates what God has not created. With dualism, the world conforms to our own image, ugly if we are divided and confused. When we do not move deeply into life, in the very principle of unity, we become ambitious, greedy, egotistical, seekers of power, position, prestige, fame. We become aggressive, brutal, violent, and overly competitive. We become the world we create. But this is not the original world that God made and "saw how good it was." Note that the Bible says, "how good it was," not "God did a good job." The world is good. Do not leave it for another world that matches to your own whims and greed. If you are against this world, you show that you are too much attached to it. Don't leave the world; rather, embrace God in it. Since God became man, the residence of the sacred became the "profane." Then the profane is no longer profane. The Incarnation changed all our understandings. God communicated Himself through the things He had created. "God so loved the world" (John 3:16). So should we. We are so much involved in the world that we know that, in practical way, there is no room for escape. Through our senses, minds, hearts, needs, and desires, we are implicated deeply in this world, with these things, and with these people. Such an implication affects and changes us, as well as affecting and changing the things and people implicated with us.

We are not alone, in this journey of reconciliation. God Himself, with His grace, continues to help us. Grace is not a kind of magical substance that enters our souls and acts like spiritual penicillin. Grace means that there is no opposition between God and His redeemed world. There is rather reconciliation and peace. There is oneness within ourselves, with God and with the world. And more – grace is sonship. It makes us the beloved sons and daughters of God and helps us to see what God meant when "God saw how good it was."

ॐ

39

Going Home

A home is not just a house. A house is a structure. A home has something more. When a house has a soul, warmth, closeness, intimacy, openness, friendship, trust, love, it becomes a home. A house is where you live without love. A home is where you live with love. When you enter someone's house, you can feel immediately whether it is simply a house or a home. Are you welcome there? Do you feel warmth, celebration, delight, vibrations of love? Then it is a home. If what they offer you is a cold structure – bricks and boards – then it is house, albiet beautifully designed and solidly constructed. Houses are dead. Homes are alive. You can buy a house, but you can never buy a home. A home is a gift, an attitude, a gratefulness, a trust. Home is the house of love.

When there is true love in your heart, people around you are at home. They feel comfortable with you. They feel comfortable also with themselves. Strangeness is re-placed by belonging, rejection by acceptance. They feel what they already are.

Only at home can growth take place because only in love is a spiritual life possible. If you have knowledge, competence, success, dreams, pleasure, notoriety, without love, you have a beautiful house, a famous address, but you are not at home there. You feel like a stranger to yourself. Productivity cannot give a sense of belonging. Success is not necessarily followed by "at homeness."

Home is being in harmony, walking on the right path, living your values, using your gifts, being happy – alone or with others, with animals and nature, in a certain city or in a certain civilization and having there that sense of "ringing true." You have harmony when your behavior and beliefs come together. When your outer life is an expression of your inner life, and when you are true to yourself, you feel at home. Home is a harmony in your spiritual center, that inner point associated with a sense of wholeness. You find this bliss whenever you feel at home, in whatever circumstances of your life, in your solitude, with others, at play, at work, in nature, in a place of worship, or in any other place and time where a warm hearth and a welcoming heart greet you.

Going home means leaving the security of our houses, roles, relationships, belief systems, lifestyles, in search of an abiding homeland – like Abraham who left his home without knowing where he was going. Only his faith in God was guiding him, and it was more than enough. Going home means to embrace a wilderness journey leaving behind "imperatives" that are no longer healthy, fulfilling, suitable. It is getting rid of old patterns, perceptions, and behaviors that no longer fit. Jesus said to His disciples, "If anyone comes to me without turning his back on his father and mother, his wife and children, his brothers and sisters, indeed his very self, he cannot be my follower" (Luke 14:26).

It is a one-way trip according to the will of God for today, not a round trip to yesterday's guarantees, assurances, and certainties. It is a letting go of those "realities" that are not really real in order to allow space for another to grow, to expand, to be. But, in another sense, it is also a round-trip to our daily lives, this time filled with God alone. And that makes a big difference.

Going home is grieving our "losses." It is a death, the death of transformation. Grieving allows a rebirth, a new "us," the freedom of the homeland. It is the re-incarnation of God in us. It is resurrection. Only then can you be at ease with yourself and with the universe. The universe becomes your own universe. At that moment you can never be anywhere other than at home. If the universe is your home, how can you be outside? In fact, where can you go? "Always home," indeed. At that moment you will accept the contours of your life and say yes to this new evolving existence without reservation, because it is the will of God. But we will feel that way only when all the accumulated nonsense inside of us is released and thrown away, and we live our true self here and now. "Now," is there any other way to live? "Here," is there another home? Beware of the illusions, the deceptions, and the mirages and keep in mind that the whole is the home and the home is nowhere. Home has no maps. At home who needs a map?

We are restless, we humans. Human beings must be restless. Only when they become one with God can inner peace happen. Before that, relaxation is not possible. This is our destiny. Our home is God, the very core of our being. This is the place where all kinds of dualities drop. This is the place that every one of us is seeking. This is the place where, when we get there, we notice that we have always been without being aware of it. We were unconscious, sleepy, alienated. Awakened, we feel universal, without boundaries, free, creative, in the very image of God. Then nothing matters. You've experienced God. You've become another Christ. At home, you become another Christ, you are a living Bible.

The human being can only be satisfied when one's house is transformed into one's home, and one's home becomes the temple of God.

ॐ

40

God Speaks – Listen

God speaks all the time, anytime, anywhere. God is even talkative, garrulous.

We do not listen.

He speaks through the events of our daily existence.

We do not listen because we prefer Him to speak our language, in our accents and according to our whims and beliefs and needs.

God's language is, according to us, the most difficult of all languages because we do not want to learn it. We do not trust His skills. We think He does not pronounce clearly and loudly, and He does not know much about straight lines and correct punctuation.

God speaks through the events and happenings of our own lives and all of life. We prefer to understand Him only in some events, the most convenient ones, in our lives.

God speaks through everyone, everyday, everywhere. But our selfishness prevents us from perceiving Him in everyone, everyday, everywhere.

God speaks all the time, anytime, anywhere.

He speaks often in whispers. Listen!

His language would be easier for us if we forget a little more of our own language, our own human calculations, and our own driving fantasies.

God's language is one of reality. Why do we keep missing it?

&

41

Treasuring All These Things in the Heart

In front of the Word of God, one usually finds oneself in one of the three following positions. One can jump for joy and say, "I got it. My heart is on fire! It is wonderful. It couldn't be better. It is magnificent. It is enlightening. I understand it. Now I see." One can also say negatively, "This is impossible to understand. I do not see anything. I do not learn anything. It does not speak to me." Or one can say with indifference, "It does not matter what it says. I am not concerned."

Attitudes and reactions range from joyful inspiration to cold indifference. Most of these attidutes are false, or at least deceitful.

The sound attitude is the ingenious one, the one taken by Mary. When she did not understand the Word of God and what Jesus was saying and what He was doing, she "kept all these things in memory" (Luke 2:51). "Mary treasured all these things and reflected on them in her heart" (Luke 2:19). This is exactly what we should do. We should keep in memory the Word of God, treasure it, reflect on it and repeat it indefinitely until it speaks to us and transforms us. It is God's breath in us.

The Mother of Jesus never preached. She did not hold any public office. She was not committed publicly to any charity actions. She did not belong to any organization or club. She did not have an official ministry of any kind. Mary kept herself in the penumbra. She let God dwell in her. She let God be.

Mary was silent; nevertheless, her presence was so eloquent, so communicative, so strong!

She stayed in her small house, in her tiny village, all her life. Nevertheless she was with her Son everywhere, at every moment.

She knew she had, in her existence, something special, sacred, and divine. She managed to respond to it through faith, fidelity, and much love. She did not understand all of what was happening. In a sense, she did not need to understand because she was sure. Her faith was total. She "kept all these things in memory." She "treasured all these things and reflected on them in her heart." And the salvation of the world spread out from that little home of that little village and transformed the universe and everything in it!